DERBY COUNTY
Thirty Memorable Games
from the Nineties

ANDY ELLIS

DERBY COUNTY
Thirty Memorable Games
from the Nineties

First published in Great Britain in 2011 by The Derby Books Publishing Company Limited, 3 The Parker Centre, Derby, DE21 4SZ.

ISBN 978-1-85983-859-4
Printed and bound by Melita Press, Malta.

CONTENTS

INTRODUCTION

The 1990s was an eventful decade for Derby County, which began in Division One under the ownership of Robert Maxwell. His unwillingness to fund the football club after finishing fifth the previous season soon had a detrimental effect on the club as there were to be no more incoming transfers and, despite local businessman Lionel Pickering being willing and able to buy the club, they could not reach agreement on the price. This ultimately led to relegation and the subsequent sale of the prized assets of Mark Wright and Dean Saunders to Liverpool in the summer of 1991.

The reduction in the club's value allowed Pickering to take control and, fortunately, the management team of Arthur Cox and Roy McFarland provided some continuity and could start the rebuilding process. Mr Pickering funded the large-scale rebuilding of the team that saw many multi-million pound transfers (Craig Short, Tommy Johnson, Paul Kitson and Marco Gabbiadini), but they rarely gelled into a consistent force.

The best they could manage was a Play-off semi-final in 1992 and a Wembley appearance in the Anglo-Italian Cup Final in 1993 where they were soundly beaten by Cremonese.

Arthur Cox was forced to resign his post due to ill health, and his natural successor was Roy McFarland who was in charge of the team that made it to the Divisional Play-off Final in 1994, unluckily being beaten by Leicester City.

Jim Smith, 'The Bald Eagle', was brought in as manager to bring some new ideas, players and new life into the club. He brought with him Oxford United reserve-team manager and former Derby player Steve McClaren as his assistant and first-team coach. Together they, along with some clever, inspired signings such as the Croatian international captain Igor Stimac, Robbie van der Laan and Ron Willems, saw promotion to the Premier League, which was achieved at the first attempt.

The Baseball Ground's days were numbered and the capacity had been reduced to 18,000, which would not be enough to fund a Premier League team, and the facilities demanded by media, corporate sponsors and fans alike pushed Derby to move to a new purpose-built stadium on the new Pride Park site.

The move to the new stadium in 1997 was a superb setting for Premier League football, and Jim Smith was able to attract further foreign stars – Stefano Eranio, Jacob Laursen, Franceso Baiano, Aljosa Asanovic and Paulo Wanchope who all pushed Derby up to eighth position in the Premier League by end of the 1998–99 season.

Things started to go wrong towards the end of the decade when Steve McClaren's ability was noticed by Manchester United, whom he joined as a coach to Alex Ferguson's team and helped them to their Treble triumph in 1999.

As the foreign stars moved on, less well known players were signed and the team struggled to maintain its Premier League status, although the transfer fees involved were ever increasing. In 10 years between 1990 and 2000 they had come a long way, and selecting 30 of the 546 matches played during the decade is not an easy task. Matches can be memorable for many reasons – the occasion, the match or the result – and some of those included in this selection did not always result in a win for Derby. Some are obvious selections, such as the two Wembley appearances, the last game at the Baseball Ground and promotion to the Premier League; others may not be so obvious, or immediately memorable.

When the reader looks at some of the games, hopefully they will recall the incidents here and bring their own memories of those particular games.

These are my choices, and I would expect that many of them will appear on most peoples' own lists, but I do hope to revive memories of some of the games and incidents during them that have made them memorable in one way or another – although not always pleasant if you are a Derby fan.

ACKNOWLEDGEMENTS

There have been lots of different resources used in compiling the information and details in this book.

They range from watching hours of old VHS video footage of individual matches and the official Derby County Season Reviews, reading match reports from the *Derby Evening Telegraph* and other national newspapers that give an overall impression of the 30 matches. Derby's own matchday programme, *The Ram*, also contains valuable information and reports for the researcher and several quotations from the manager at the time.

My own Derby County Database was the source of all of the statistical information, and a number of other Derby County reference books have filled in the remaining gaps:

Player of the Year – Jim Fearn

Journey through a Season – Ian Hall

Who's Who of Derby County – Gerald Mortimer

All of the photographs are taken from my personal collection and are unattributed on the reverse, so I'm unable to trace the copyright holder in order to acknowledge them individually. The exception being Geraint Williams, which is credited to David Munden.

Thanks to Andy Appleby, chairman of Derby County, for his opening remarks and the rest of the staff at Pride Park, that I have regular contact with, for their continued support.

Obviously, none of this would be possible without the backing of Steve and Alex at Derby Books Publishing, who guided me through, once again.

My thanks as always to my father, John, for his suggestions and corrections and, finally, to my wife Jenny and daughters Naomi and Katie, both Rams fans (whether they want to be or not!).

FOREWORD

Being a part of the Derby County family has been a tremendous honour and privilege. Andy's commitment to the Rams' rich history is second to none, and this latest book continues to add to a moving body of work. I have no doubt that every Rams supporter remembers each and every one of these 30 memorable matches, from the two Wembley visits, to the close of the Baseball Ground and the move to Pride Park. Our club has experienced a great number of memorable moments over these past 126 years, and I look forward to many more.... of our heart and our soul, we're searching for glory, and victory is our goal.

Andy Appleby,
Chairman,
Derby County

DERBY COUNTY 6
SUNDERLAND 0

League Cup   **Wednesday 31 October 1990**

Baseball Ground

Derby County: Shilton, Sage, Cross, G. Williams, Wright, Forsyth, Micklewhite, Saunders, Harford, Ramage, Pickering. Subs: Gee, Briscoe.
Sunderland: Norman, Kay, Smith (Cullen, 53), Bennett (Ord, 45), Ball, Owers, Bracewell, Armstrong, Davenport, Gabbiadini, Hardyman.
Referee: K.S. Hackett (Sheffield)
Attendance: 16,422

Derby played against Sunderland in the League Cup competition on the same date some 17 years previously, with Sunderland winning by a 3–0 margin. This was in a second replay just two days after the first. Arthur Cox at that time was Sunderland's assistant manager and Roy McFarland was playing in the Derby team.

Things were very different 17 years later – Derby had just won their first League game of the season, an away win at Southampton thanks to a goal from Mick Harford. Derby's only change to that winning team was to replace Nigel Callaghan with former Sunderland utility player, Nick Pickering. Callaghan was now in his second spell with Derby and this was an enforced change, with his parent club, Aston Villa, not allowing him to become Cup tied while they were still in the competition.

Despite the terrible start to the season, Derby were unbeaten in three games, winning two and drawing one. Arthur Cox was still in hospital following a nasal operation, and he had left managerial matters in the hands of Roy McFarland. The change of voice and methods, on a temporary basis at least, had an immediate effect, with the Rams winning at Southampton in his first game in charge.

Sunderland had found themselves unexpectedly promoted at the end of the previous season, despite losing to the Play-off winners Swindon Town. Swindon's off-the-field issues were punished by the League by blocking their promotion.

Both teams had managed just one League win between them in the 16 games played which, not unexpectedly, found both of them in the bottom four and looking for some Cup success.

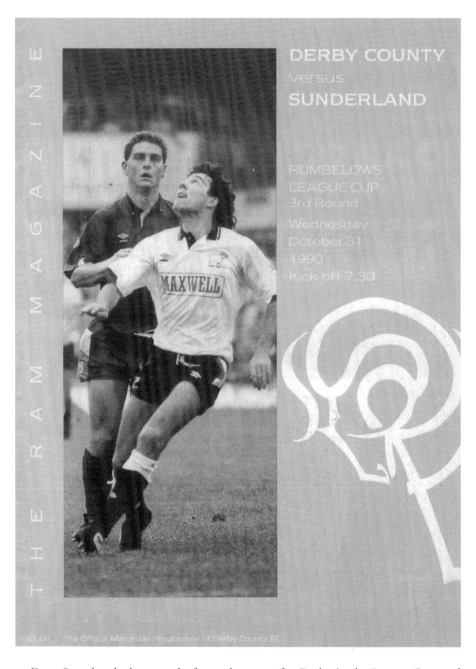

Dean Saunders had a record of a goal a game for Derby in the League Cup, and Sunderland's main forward threat was Marco Gabbiadini who had scored twice in the previous round and was on six goals for the season so far. In the previous round Derby struggled to overcome Carlisle United 2–1 on aggregate, while Sunderland won 6–1 at Bristol City after losing 0–1 in the home leg.

There were a number of Sunderland connections in the Derby team – Mick Harford was a lifelong fan, Nick Pickering was a former player and had played in the League Cup Final for them and Arthur Cox was the coach when Sunderland beat Leeds United in the 1973 FA Cup Final.

Derby kicked-off playing towards the Osmaston End of the Baseball Ground, packed full of the travelling north east fans. The first chance of the night went to the main danger man Gabbiadini. He out-muscled Mark Wright and then created himself a couple of yards of space before shooting from 25 yards out. His shot was all along the ground and, with Shilton diving full length to his left, was inches wide.

The positive start by both teams in the first 10 minutes continued with Derby's first opportunity coming from Saunders. A quick, first-time ball from Sage to Saunders gave him the opportunity to turn his marker Bennett quickly and immediately shoot from 30 yards from goal. The powerful shot was on target and tipped over by the goalkeeper Norman. If anything, the shot was too near the middle of the goal, where the goalkeeper was standing; a couple of yards either side and he would have had no chance of keeping the ball out.

The resulting Micklewhite corner was aimed at Harford, who jumped with two defenders 12 yards from goal. Although he did not get a vast amount of power in this header, it looped over everyone and beat the defender on the post and nestled in the back of the net.

Two minutes later Derby doubled their lead. From a Shilton goal-kick, Harford did well to win the ball and immediately sent Micklewhite off down the right wing. As he approached the edge of the penalty area, he fired over a low, hard cross along the edge of the goal area. Bennett tried to knock the ball out for a corner but mis-timed his attempt and the ball went the wrong side of the post into the net, with the goalkeeper diving to catch the original cross.

Sunderland had a golden opportunity to get back into the game with Gabbiadini as the most likely player to score. Sage lost possession to Hardyman whose cross picked out an unmarked Owers, who headed back to Gabbiadini. Mark Wright, learning from his earlier challenge with Gabbiadini, was stronger this time and just did enough to put him off. Sunderland were enjoying some good possession but had little opportunity in the final third where Gabbiadini was left largely on his own and unsupported.

Derby's third goal on 35 minutes started from a Sunderland throw inside the Derby half, and within a matter of seconds and five passes later the ball was in the Sunderland net. The wayward throw only found Forsyth, and a succession of first-time passes from Forsyth, Saunders and Williams reached the right wing again and the ever energetic Micklewhite. As he was closed down by two defenders he sent a long cross-field ball towards Harford, who out jumped the full-back to send another looping header into the net at the far post.

Shortly afterwards it was nearly 4–0 as a combination of Micklewhite, Sage and Saunders carved an opening for Pickering, who came sliding in. Bennett was alert to the possible danger and just managed to get there first and give away a corner.

On 43 minutes, any doubt about the result was removed with Derby's fourth goal and Harford's third, following some excellent movement and running off the ball. The move started on the edge of Derby's penalty area when Micklewhite broke up an attack. He passed to Saunders and set off at pace down his usual wing and, as he passed halfway, Williams found him with a pass, and he sent over a first-time ball deep into the penalty area. The ball did not have quite enough power to get beyond the full-back, John Kay, who could not direct it sufficiently towards his goalkeeper and Harford came from behind him to lash the ball left footed past Norman from eight yards.

Derby had not previously scored more than one goal in any game this season and had booked their place in the next round by half-time. The Sunderland fans, though, were far from happy, as indeed was manager Dennis Smith, who replaced Bennett with Ord at the interval.

Derby continued to create chances, with Pickering taking a shot from the edge of the penalty area that was just wide and Harford continued his dominance of the central defenders. Their fifth goal on 51 minutes was probably their best of the season, featuring eight different players and no Sunderland player touching the ball until it nestled in the net. Starting from Shilton's punt downfield, the ball was moved from the right touchline (Harford) across the field by interchanging passes between Ramage, Sage, Williams, Forsyth, Saunders and Cross. The ball arrived with Saunders on the left wing, and he passed square to Forsyth who had come up from the back and in some space played a short pass to Ramage on the penalty area line. Ramage turned, all alone, took one touch and placed the ball to Norman's left. This was only the 20-year-old's second goal for Derby. Some Sunderland players were looking for an offside, but the referee was perfectly placed and could see that the left-back was the last defender.

At 5–0 Derby relaxed a little, and this allowed Sunderland to play a bit more, and their best opportunity came when Wright missed a tackle and allowed a cross to come over to Owers who was in a lot of space. Even though he got power to his header, he could not direct it past Shilton, who got down well to save.

On 66 minutes another defensive error led to Derby's sixth goal. Pickering played the ball to Saunders, with his back to goal, and as he checked back the defender slipped, leaving Saunders one on one against Norman. Normally, Saunders would be expected to shoot and score from that position, especially as he was not on the scoresheet yet;

however, as the covering defender came over he touched the ball to his right and found Ramage waiting to bury the ball with his left foot.

With over 20 minutes left, Sunderland and their noisy fans could only have been dreading the scoreline at the end of the game. And Micklewhite nearly scored the goal of his career with a superb goal, running with the ball for a large part of the field, mainly because none of the Sunderland midfield or defenders tried to stop him, and his final left-foot shot was tipped over.

For a team sitting near the bottom of the League table, Derby gave a remarkable performance, with a couple of outstanding individual performances from Mick Harford (who not only scored three goals but was a constant threat) and Gary Micklewhite (his pace and crossing from the right side produced a number of goals and opportunities).

Steve Cross was playing just his third game since returning from the horrific injury sustained in the same competition at West Ham United in 1989 and earned special praise from the manager – 'playing with so much enthusiasm, ability and will to win'.

The following League game Derby beat Luton Town and then drew with Manchester United but after that only won four more games all season as they found themselves in a relegation fight. In the next round of the competition Derby went out to Sheffield Wednesday, losing 1–2 at home after a 1–1 draw at Hillsborough.

Within a year, Marco Gabbiadini had signed for Derby from Crystal Palace after his big-money move to the capital did not work out for him.

MICK HARFORD

Born: 12 February 1959
Debut v Nottingham Forest (home), Division One, 20 January 1990, lost 0–2
Last game v Barnsley (home), Division Two, 7 September 1991, draw 1–1
First goal v Tottenham Hotspur (home), Division One, 24 February 1990, won 2–1
Bought from: Luton Town
Sold to: Luton Town
Total appearances: 68, 18 goals
Consecutive games: 31 from 20 January 1990 to 31 October 1990

Mick Harford is regarded as Luton Town's best-ever player and earned two England caps for his ability as an old-fashioned English centre-forward. He helped Luton win the League Cup in 1988 and also scored in the Final a year later.

Paul Goddard had the opportunity to move back south to Millwall and Harford was brought in as his replacement for a fee of £450,000 in January 1990. His partnership with Dean Saunders never really clicked in the way it was hoped. Following the relegation and Maxwell's refusal to invest further, Harford was re-sold to Luton for £325,000 in September 1991, despite approaches from Manchester United.

DERBY COUNTY 4
CHELSEA 6

Division One Saturday 15 December 1990

Baseball Ground

Derby County: Shilton, Sage, Pickering, Ramage (P. Williams, 55), Wright, Forsyth, Micklewhite, Saunders, Harford, Hebberd, Callaghan. Other sub: Gee.
Chelsea: Beasant, Hall, Dorigo, Stuart, Cundy, Monkou (Nicholas, 57), Le Saux, Lee, Dixon, Durie, Wise (Wilson, 89).
Referee: I.J. Borrett (Harleston)
Attendance: 15,057

Derby had lost one of the previous seven games while Chelsea had won their last five games in all competitions, so it had the potential to be a good, open game. The teams had met on the opening day of the season, when Chelsea narrowly won 2–1, but largely due to the Chelsea goalkeeper Dave Beasant saving a Dean Saunders penalty-kick. Derby were still without Ted McMinn who was back in hospital having further surgery on his knee following the injury sustained at Tottenham more than 12 months previously.

In the week prior to the game Derby took part in the Guinness Soccer Six tournament held at the G-Mex Centre in Manchester. They did well, losing the Play-off match 0–1 to Luton Town, who eventually won the overall tournament.

Derby made two changes from the mid-week League Cup defeat to Sheffield Wednesday, with Mel Sage replacing Mark Patterson at right-back and Nigel Callaghan being restored to the wing. It did not take Chelsea long to break the deadlock. On 11 minutes, Gordon Durie was on the Chelsea right wing in front of the Ley Stand. He was up against Nick Pickering and was too strong for the Derby defender, turning him before skipping past Nigel Callaghan. He broke into the penalty area and fired a ball across the goal area to find Kerry Dixon unmarked at the far post to knock the ball past Shilton.

Derby were soon on level terms in what was a lively opening 15 minutes. A corner on Derby's right could only be headed behind by Chelsea's scorer, Dixon, for another

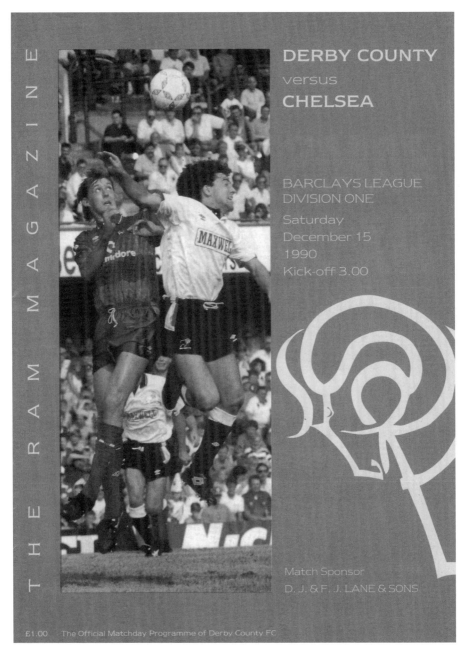

THE RAM MAGAZINE

DERBY COUNTY
versus
CHELSEA

BARCLAYS LEAGUE
DIVISION ONE
Saturday
December 15
1990
Kick-off 3.00

Match Sponsor
D. J. & F. J. LANE & SONS

£1.00   The Official Matchday Programme of Derby County FC

corner from the opposite side, this time to be taken by Callaghan. It was hit long and found Mark Wright, who could not get any power but was able to direct the ball back into the centre. Mick Harford was the quickest to react and was given time to turn and chip the ball goalwards, where it was met by the ever-lively Dean Saunders who glanced his header wide of Beasant, who was left flat footed in the centre of the goal.

Two goals in a three-minute spell just before half-time should have settled the game. A silly free-kick was given away on Derby's left, in much the same position from which Durie created the first goal from. Dennis Wise took the kick to the far post, where Harford and Forsyth got in each other's way as they were marking their respective forwards. Neither could get a firm head on the ball as it dropped back into the penalty area and found David Lee running in. He took the ball past Sage before hitting a shot that Shilton could only push into the path of Kerry Dixon to tap in his second goal of the game.

Things got worse for Derby shortly afterwards by some more poor defending not clearing the ball when they had the chance. Derby had a throw down by their own corner flag, which they did not clear. Firstly, Trevor Hebberd picked up the ball and ran with it for too long, instead of clearing the ball downfield. He lost the ball, and when it broke to Pickering he played a dangerous-looking ball back into the centre to Mark Wright who was immediately surrounded by three Chelsea players and lost the ball to Stuart. Durie found Hall in space on the right, and he fired the ball low and hard and Durie, running in, shot past Shilton with ease.

As half-time came, the Derby players and management would have been disappointed with their defending in general, and particularly letting in two avoidable goals so close to the break.

Ten minutes into the second half, Derby made a telling substitution, bringing on Paul Williams in place of Craig Ramage, and they managed to get themselves back into the game shortly afterwards with a goal from Trevor Hebberd. A Mel Sage free-kick on halfway was flicked on by Harford and fell to Wright, but he could not get his foot to the ball before it was cleared as far as Callaghan on the left wing, in front of the C-Stand. He drew the defenders, and that allowed space for Pickering to cross the ball to find Harford, who was able to head the ball down for Hebberd to run round the back of the defence and score from six yards.

Chelsea seemed to have lost concentration, and very shortly after the Hebberd goal Derby got a deserved equaliser. A series of passes between Hebberd and Pickering found Callaghan on the touchline. He very quickly took one touch and swung over a cross with his right foot and his perfect delivery found Saunders, who had dropped behind his marker and made room for himself. His header was planted to Beasant's right hand side to pull the game level at 3–3.

There was better to come for Derby as they turned a 1–3 scoreline at half-time to a 4–3 advantage with three goals in space of 13 minutes. Williams, showing his tackling ability in midfield and his driving runs, won a throw on the touch line in front of the dug outs.

The ball came back to Williams and his forward movement and pass found Saunders on the edge of the area, back to goal. Despite having some close attention from three defenders, he was allowed to turn and chipped the ball over them. A deflection off Nicholas saw the ball reach the unmarked Micklewhite who hit the ball first time past Beasant to complete a remarkable turnaround in fortunes.

It was a massively entertaining game for the neutral fans, a roller coaster of emotions for both sets of fans and a nightmare for the managers and coaches whose instructions did not seem to have any effect on those playing. Instead of sitting back and making Chelsea do all the work, Derby were still trying to score more goals and leaving themselves open to counter attacks from the pacy Chelsea forwards. What we were witnessing was some very good attacking play and passing interchanges but very poor positional play and defending from both sides.

Derby nearly had a fifth goal as some one-touch passing between Harford, Williams, Saunders and Micklewhite combined to set Hebberd free running through the centre of the Chelsea defence, being chased by Wise. His shot was tipped away for a corner. From the Callaghan corner on Derby's left, the ball fell to Stuart on the edge of his own area. He was allowed to run, unchallenged past halfway, and his pass found Durie out on the right wing, in a similar amount of open space. As Trevor Hebberd ran back to challenge, Durie took one look up and sent over a cross. Mark Wright was left all alone in the defence with four Chelsea forwards, and it was the unmarked Dennis Wise whose header easily beat Shilton to level the scores again at 4–4.

Derby to failed to learn their lesson from the last Chelsea goal, and from yet another Derby corner Beasant's quick throw out to Durie, this time operating on the left, left the home defence exposed again. Durie was left to run unchallenged for half the length of the field. As he reached the Derby area, he cut inside, and although there were four defenders between him and the goal, he shot all along the ground and into the corner of Shilton's net: 4–5!

As the game moved into injury time, and with Derby throwing men forward trying for another equaliser, there was always the possibility of another Chelsea attack. Dorigo picked the ball up deep in his own half and was allowed to run a long way upfield. His ball out wide to Stuart allowed him into the area, and as Sage came over to tackle him he cut the ball back for a young Graeme Le Saux to score at the near post: 4–6 !

There was just time to kick-off again before the referee blew for full-time. The result left Derby in 15th place spoiling a run of four wins from the last six games. The defensive failings during this game were to plague them throughout the season. The 4–6 scoreline was only the second time that a home game had ended in such a way; the other one was against Sheffield Wednesday in November 1927.

Arthur Cox commented afterwards that 'one thing missing from the game, showing all things good about British football, on both sides, was the art of individual and collective defending...The majority of the 10 goals scored could be traced back to one or more individual errors...disappointed and embarrassed to score four goals at home and still lose the match.'

'Having fought back to a 4–3 lead with 12 minutes to go, the excitement and noise generated by the crowd overtook the player's common sense'

MARK WRIGHT

Born: 1 August 1963
Debut v Wimbledon (home), Division One, 29 August 1987, lost 0–1
Last game v Luton Town (away), Division One, 11 May 1991, lost 0–2
First goal v Watford (home), Division One, 5 December 1987, draw 1–1
Bought from: Southampton
Sold to: Liverpool
Total appearances: 171, 10 goals
Consecutive appearances: 32 from 17 March 1990 to 15 December 1990

Mark Wright started his professional career in 1980 at Oxford United, making just 10 appearances before moving to Southampton in 1982. Arthur Cox spent £760,000 on the central defender on 8 August 1987 as Derby were looking to build on their new Division One status and made his debut on 29 August in a 0–1 home defeat against Wimbledon. He was to form a formidable spine of Shilton, Wright and Saunders in a new-look team.

A footballing centre-half, Wright's form for Derby saw him break into the England team as a successor to Terry Butcher, and he was selected in the England World Cup squad for the Italia '90 Finals, scoring against Egypt in the 64th minute of a group stage game. He played in all the games apart from the first group match as England reached the semi-finals.

As a natural leader, he was named as captain and led Derby to their highest League finish since being champions in 1974–75 when they finished fifth in the 1988–89 season. He was twice voted as Player of the Year.

Chairman Robert Maxwell's refusal to keep funding the club meant that to begin paying him back for his investments Wright was sold to Liverpool on 15 July 1991 for £2.5 million (then a record transfer fee for a defender), following Derby's relegation to Division Two. Dean Saunders followed just four days later. At Liverpool, he captained

them to an FA Cup Final success in the 1992 competition. He pulled on a Derby shirt again in May 2006, playing in his good friend Ted McMinn's benefit game in front of a record attendance for a game at Pride Park.

DERBY COUNTY 1
LIVERPOOL 7

Division One   **Saturday 23 March 1991**

Baseball Ground

Derby County: Shilton, Sage, Cross, G. Williams, Wright, Forsyth, Micklewhite, Saunders, Harford, Wilson (Hebberd, 54), McMinn. Other sub: Patterson.
Liverpool: Hooper, Hysen, Burrows, Nicol, Molby (Staunton, 54), Ablett, Beardsley, Houghton, Rush, Barnes, Gillespie. Other sub: Speedie.
Referee: P. Don (Hanworth Park)
Attendance: 20,531

Liverpool were lying second in the League, level on points with Arsenal (who had an inferior goal difference), with Crystal Palace in third place, some five points behind. Derby were looking doomed to relegation, bottom of the League and some 10 points behind the third-bottom team, Southampton. Mick Harford, after missing the defeat at Crystal Palace, returned to lead the front line, and that in turn meant that Trevor Hebberd would drop to the bench. Derby had gone 12 games since their last League win, which was an away at Sunderland at the beginning of December, so based on current form Liverpool were the clear favourites.

It took Liverpool just seven minutes to take the lead, resulting from poor defensive positioning. A Peter Shilton goal-kick barely reached the centre circle and was immediately headed back over the Derby defence which was pushing out. Ian Rush, in the prime of his Liverpool career, found himself goal side of the defence with Mark Wright closing. Wright made a clumsy challenge in the penalty area, where he was fortunate to escape the red card for a professional foul on the striker. Jan Molby (who had scored four penalties already during the season) stepped forward, and his long straight run gave the 'keeper no clue as to where the ball was going. Shilton dived the right way, but the kick was well placed in the corner.

A second penalty-kick was awarded on 20 minutes, this time to Derby. Ian Wilson (formerly of Leicester City and signed on loan from Besitkas) won the ball in midfield and passed to McMinn in space out in the left channel. Mike Hooper (in goal for the injured Bruce Grobbelaar) rushed out to McMinn, who had cleverly pushed the ball

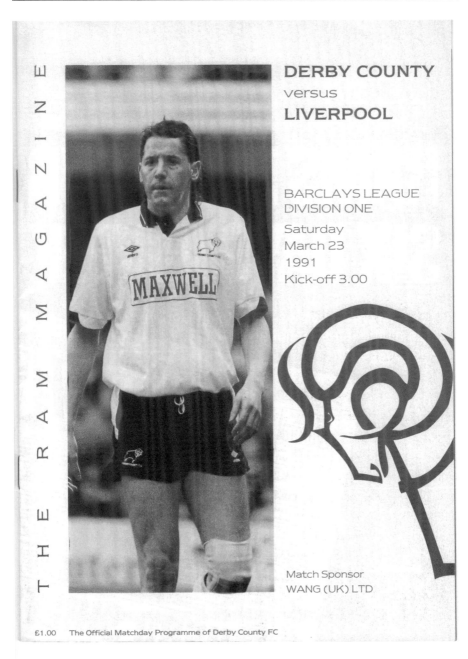

THE RAM MAGAZINE

DERBY COUNTY
versus
LIVERPOOL

BARCLAYS LEAGUE
DIVISION ONE
Saturday
March 23
1991
Kick-off 3.00

Match Sponsor
WANG (UK) LTD

£1.00   The Official Matchday Programme of Derby County FC

past him, and inevitably brought the Derby forward down, leaving the referee no option but to give the penalty-kick. The goalkeeper picked up a yellow card, escaping a sending off by virtue of the fact that McMinn was not able to score from his position.

Dean Saunders took the kick and Hooper, obviously caught in two minds which way to dive, did nothing and stood and watched as he placed the ball into the bottom left of his goal for his 18th goal of the season. That would be the last the Derby strikers would see of the ball as the players were largely chasing shadows for the rest of the game and the midfield were unable to get the ball forward.

They were only level for three minutes as the Derby midfield and defence were out thought and out-manoeuvred. Molby was given too much time to play the ball over the midfield area to Peter Beardsley, who took the ball past Forsyth. A one-two between Barnes and Rush left Rush isolated again against Wright as he tried to side foot the ball past Shilton from 12 yards. Shilton got down to it, but could only push the ball into the path of John Barnes who could not miss.

For all Derby's running and undoubted effort, they could not find a way through the midfield area to get the ball to the forwards and the game was really over, even at 1–2. Liverpool further extended their lead before the break, the familiar trio of Barnes, Beardsley and Rush involved again. Barnes, on the left wing this time, played the ball to Beardsley in the penalty area who was being tracked by Forsyth. A clever piece of skill from the England international created an extra yard of space required for him to fire over a low cross which was met by Rush just three yards out to score his 22nd goal of the season.

It was hard to see what the management could do at half-time to turn things around, other than to try and limit the amount of space given to the Liverpool midfield.

Liverpool were now attacking the Osmaston End, where their own fans were standing, and did not take long to give them a closer view of a goal. Mel Sage, still trying to get forward and get some service to his forwards, was caught in possession and the ball played to Beardsley in the space vacated by Sage. This time it was Barnes who was on the end of the pass, and his pace and strength took him past Wright and Forsyth and his first time shot beat Shilton at his near post: 1–4. From Derby's point of view, it was now a damage limitation exercise, with Hebberd coming on to replace Wilson in the middle. It made little difference.

Liverpool's next goal was a little fortunate – Barnes again found space behind Sage, all on his own with his back to goal. He was allowed to turn and was faced by three Derby defenders. He was given time to look around and play the ball back to the penalty area 'D' where he had picked out Steve Nicol, whose shot took a big deflection and beat everyone to end up in the net: 1–5.

Some Derby fans began drifting home, realising it was now getting embarrassing. Six minutes after the fifth goal Liverpool sliced through the defence again to score a sixth. The movement of the Liverpool forwards had created space on Derby's right, as Sage had followed Barnes into the penalty area. Nicol was the player to profit this time and had time to line up his shot and for the second time in the half, Shilton was beaten at his near post, which is one of the basic things a goalkeeper is taught.

This was already Liverpool's biggest win against Derby for nearly 60 years, when they won 6–1 on 19 November 1932 – but that was at Anfield.

Just a few minutes from the end and Liverpool completed the scoring when Houghton played a ball to Barnes who back-heeled it and that caught the Derby defence out completely and Houghton, who had continued running found himself in the same position as Barnes and Nicol did for their goals. Having conceded two goals at his near post, Shilton would not want that to happen again and probably left a bigger gap to aim at the far post – exactly where Houghton placed it to make the score 7–1 to the visitors.

This was Derby's biggest defeat since they lost at home to Middlesbrough on 29 August 1959, by the same scoreline. It was now 13 games since a League win, and the club were well adrift at the foot of the table with just four wins and were some 12 points from safety and with a much worse goal difference. Liverpool's win allowed them to leapfrog over Arsenal to go a point clear at the top of the table.

After this defeat, the players management, staff and supporters would not be looking forward to the next home game – against Arsenal, challenging for the title, who would be the eventual champions. Arthur Cox said that it was not a pleasant experience for all concerned and admitted that the two goals conceded before half-time, apart from the dubious penalty, were of international quality. *Sunday Mirror's* Alan Thompson reported that, 'the Liverpool mean machine rolled menacingly back into top gear to crush poor Derby. In fairness to Derby, very few defences in the world would have found an answer to the brilliance of England duo John Barnes and Peter Bearsdley in this mood.'

DEAN SAUNDERS

Born: 21 June 1964
Debut v Wimbledon (home), Division One, 29 October 1988, won 4–1
Last game v Luton Town (away), Division One, 11 May 1991, lost 0–2
First goal v Wimbledon (home), Division One, 29 October 1988, won 4–1
Bought from: Oxford United
Sold to: Liverpool
Total appearances: 131, 56 goals
Consecutive games: 130 from 5 November 1988 to 11 May 1991

Saunders started his career at his home-town club Swansea City, where his father had also been a player. Moves to Cardiff City on loan and Brighton brought him to the

attention of Division One strugglers Oxford United in 1987, where he helped them avoid relegation.

Derby were in need of a regular goalscorer, only scoring 35 in 40 League games during the previous season, their first back in the top flight. Saunders became Derby's first £1 million pound player when he signed in October 1988, in a transfer that caused the Oxford manager Mark Lawrenson to be sacked for complaining about the transfer between father and son of the Maxwell family.

He made his debut on 29 October 1988 against Wimbledon in a First Division fixture at the Baseball Ground. He made an immediate impact at his new club, scoring twice in his first game. In his first season he scored 14 goals in 30 games. His goals helped the Rams finish an impressive fifth in the 1988–89 First Division table, playing alongside Paul Goddard – their highest finish since they were League champions in 1975 – but they were unable to compete in the UEFA Cup due to the ban on English teams in European competition. He added 11 League goals to his name in 1989–90, but Derby slumped to 16th place. With the club for sale and relegated, his departure was inevitable, and he followed Mark Wright to Liverpool for £2.9 million to partner Ian Rush. He missed one game in his three years at the club – a League Cup game for which he was inelligible.

MANCHESTER CITY 2
DERBY COUNTY 1

Division One   **Saturday 20 April 1991**

Maine Road

Manchester City: Coton, Hill, Pointon, Heath, Hendry, Redmond, White, Brennan, Quinn, Harper, Ward (Reid, 75). Other sub: Allen.
Derby County: M. Taylor, Sage, Pickering, G. Williams, Wright, Kavanagh (Cross, 80), Micklewhite, Saunders, Harford, Wilson (Patterson, 40), P. Williams.
Referee: K.A. Lupton (Stockton)
Attendance: 24,037

Derby's position at the bottom meant that defeat in this match would mean certain relegation to Division Two. Unusually, the fixture list had given Derby five successive away games – Queen's Park Rangers, Nottingham Forest, Coventry City, Manchester United and now Manchester City.

Most of the blame for the current position did not lie with the management team of Cox and McFarland but with the chairman, Robert Maxwell, who refused to put any more money into the club to fund new players, preferring to divert money into his ailing business empire. All this after finishing fifth two seasons previously, which included beating the champions Arsenal home and away.

Derby's defence was changing on a weekly basis and the latest change was enforced, with Forsyth who was playing alongside Mark Wright being ruled out for the rest of the season, and replaced by Jason Kavanagh. This allowed Nick Pickering to come in at left-back.

Manchester City had appointed Peter Reid as player-manager in November, and he was still looking to make his mark and impress. City started brightly with some excellent approach play that would please the manager, who had named himself as one of the substitutes. This movement between the forwards meant that Derby's defence was getting pulled all over the place, and it was really only a matter of time before City scored. The combination of the pace of White and the height of Quinn were always going to be a handful for the patched up defence.

An early opportunity came to Quinn as he and Pointon exchanged passes, and Pointon's cross was met by the diving Quinn from some way out which went straight to

BARCLAYS
LEAGUE
DIVISION
ONE

MANCHESTER CITY

versus
DERBY
COUNTY
SATURDAY,
20th
APRIL,
1991.
KICK-OFF:
3.00 p.m.

OFFICIAL
MATCH
MAGAZINE
£1.00

Martin Taylor in the Derby goal, who was making just his sixth appearance of the season.

The first goal came when a free-kick in the City half was taken by Redmond but was only headed up in the air by Kavanagh, playing in central defence as Forsyth's replacement. The ball flicked back by Ward to Quinn on the edge of the area in a central position. For a big man, Quinn had very good control and balance and caught the ball on the volley with a left-foot shot that beat all the defenders and goalkeeper Taylor.

City continued to press forward and it was hard to see where a Derby goal was going to come from unless it was from a set piece. As this was a game they had to win, the players did not seem to have ability to take the game to City and force the pace.

Another City attack was broken up by Wright, and Pickering knocked the ball over the top of the City defence as they were pushing up towards the halfway line. Dean Saunders, however, timed his run perfectly and was first to the ball in an on-side position and had a clear run on goal. He had a long way to run and a lot of time to think about what to do with the ball when he got within shooting range. Saunders took the ball round the City goalkeeper Tony Coton and was brought down for a definite penalty-kick and a possible lifeline into the game. Pointon was not happy with the linesman in front of the main stand as he did not agree with the lack of an offside flag.

The 1990–91 season brought a change in the rules for various offences and fouls, and under these new rules, the referee had the option of sending off the goalkeeper for serious foul play. The rule was still in its infancy and had only been used a couple of times against goalkeepers in the season. Referee Lupton showed the 'keeper the red card and there was obviously an uproar from the City players, especially Coton. He threw his gloves towards the referee and was reluctant to leave the field. To the relief of the Derby defence, Niall Quinn took the goalkeeper's shirt and gloves and went in goal.

After a significant delay Saunders seemed unsettled as he hit his spot-kick and Quinn, for such a tall man was able to get down quickly and turn the ball out for a corner. If Derby's relegation was in any doubt – that one shot at goal could have sealed it in one go.

Ian Wilson, again struggling in midfield, was replaced by Mark Patterson before half-time to add some more urgency and tackling to the midfield. As happened on this day, and on many times since then, Derby just seem incapable of playing against 10 men and being unable to break them down.

One thing that you need to do with a stand-in goalkeeper is to fire in shots at him. Unfortunately for Derby, they were unable to muster any shots for Quinn to deal with. Despite them being one player down, it was the home side who continued to create chances, almost at will, with the Derby midfield and forward line showing little as an attacking force.

For all their possession, City still had just the one goal to their name until a poor pass from substitute Mark Patterson was attempted to Jason Kavanagh in the centre. White, using his pace, easily intercepted the ball and was then clear of the Derby defenders. He took one touch and shot immediately from an angle into the net.

As the game was drawing to its inevitable conclusion, Derby eventually created a chance and scored. After a good spell of possession, possibly as a result of the City players getting tired from playing with 10 men for 70 minutes, Gary Micklewhite forced a throw deep in the opposition half which was worked to substitute Steve Cross. His left-foot chip into the centre found Harford all alone as the defenders stood watching. Quinn did not spot any danger quickly enough, and by the time he got to Harford's position the Derby forward had dived and headed the ball into the corner.

Shortly afterwards, the game was over, and as the reality of relegation sank in the Derby players made their way over to their fans behind the goal to thank them for their backing throughout this game and the season. This was to be the only relegation suffered during the 1990s.

The Manchester City game saw the last appearance by loanee Ian Wilson, whose 10 games saw just three draws achieved and rarely showed the form that made Everton buy him from Leicester City.

The back pages of the Sunday papers were occupied with the 42-year-old George Foreman's boxing performance against Evander Holyfield, lasting all 12 rounds before losing on points, while Derby's demise was hidden on the inside. Much of the comment was naturally reserved for Niall Quinn and his one man show and also much speculation regarding the future of Dean Saunders, who it was assumed would be leaving. Everton, Liverpool and Arsenal were all mentioned as serious contenders for his signature.

During the close season, Chairman Maxwell sold Mark Wright and Dean Saunders to Liverpool to supplement his ailing business empire and did not give Arthur Cox any of the £5 million-plus to replace those key players.

GERAINT 'GEORGE' WILLIAMS

Born: 5 January 1962
Debut v Brentford (away), Division Three, 30 March 1985, draw 1–1
Last game v Cambridge United (home), Division Two, 1 April 1992, draw 0–0
First goal v Rotherham United (away), Division Three, 2 November 1985, draw 1–1
Bought from: Bristol Rovers
Sold to: Ipswich Town
Total appearances: 330+2 subs, 10 goals
Consecutive games: 100 from 9 November 1988 to 24 November 1990

Arthur Cox had noticed Williams play for Bristol Rovers when they played at the Baseball Ground, and his midfield qualities shone. He had played over 140 games for Bristol Rovers and had been capped by Wales at Under-21 level.

On 29 March 1985, deadline day, Derby paid £40,000 for his services. His midfield partnership with John Gregory helped Derby County win promotion to the Second Division in 1986 and to the First Division a year later. He was superbly consistent and rarely missed a game in his seven years at the club and was rightly named Player of the Year for the 1986–87 season.

Derby struggled to maintain their Division One status and were relegated in 1990–91, and Williams took over the captaincy

of the team. Premier League new boys, Ipswich Town, paid £650,000 for him in July 1992. He won 11 full Wales caps with Derby.

DERBY COUNTY 6
SOUTHAMPTON 2

Division One   **Saturday 4 May 1991**

Baseball Ground

Derby County: Shilton, Sage, Forsyth, G. Williams, Wright (Kavanagh, 21), Phillips, Micklewhite, Saunders, Harford, P. Williams, McMinn. Other sub: Hebberd.
Southampton: Flowers, Horne (Kenna, 67), Adams, Cockerill, Ruddock, Gittens, Le Tissier, Maddison, Shearer, McLoughlin, Rod Wallace. Other sub: Gotsmanov.
Referee: T.J. Holbrook (Walsall)
Attendance: 11,680

Having had their relegation confirmed a couple of weeks previously, the pressure was now off the Derby players and coming into the game one hoped for a more relaxed performance. After missing the previous three games, Peter Shilton returned to face his former club, exactly 25 years to the day since he made his League debut for Leicester City against Everton.

The Player of the Year trophy was awarded before kick-off in a departure from the previous years when the announcement and presentation had been made during a supporters' awards night event. This year Dean Saunders collected his award from Arthur Cox for his 18 goals (to date) in the otherwise disappointing season.

Gary Micklewhite was playing his 200th League game for the club, and he would have played many more but for two serious injuries keeping him sidelined for long periods of time during his six and a half years with Derby.

Justin Phillips, who had made his debut in a midweek defeat to Leeds United, 11 days previously, retained his place in the centre of the defence alongside Mark Wright. Paul Williams, who was making only his fourth start having missed three months of the season with a knee injury, was handed a starting place supporting Dean Saunders and Mick Harford in attack.

Southampton were struggling in Division One, mainly a result of their away form which had seen them lose 12 away games so far, and it was only on 20 April that they were mathematically safe from relegation. Their forward line featured Matt le Tissier and a young Alan Shearer who had played for the England Under-21 team during the season.

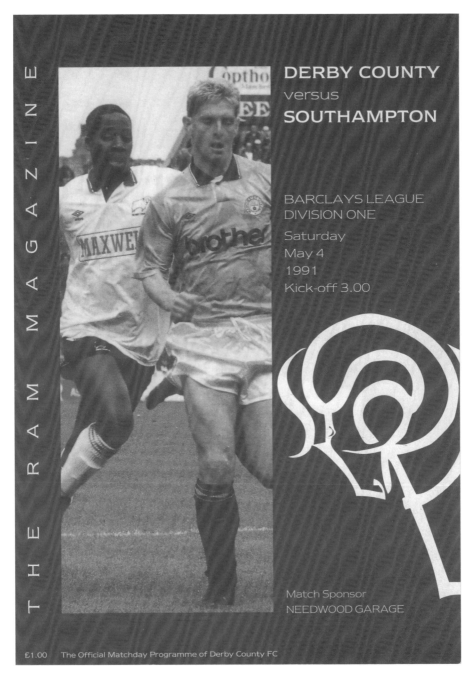

THE RAM MAGAZINE

DERBY COUNTY
versus
SOUTHAMPTON

BARCLAYS LEAGUE
DIVISION ONE
Saturday
May 4
1991
Kick-off 3.00

Match Sponsor
NEEDWOOD GARAGE

£1.00　　The Official Matchday Programme of Derby County FC

Derby had a perfect start on four minutes, when the combination of Harford, Saunders and Paul Williams worked immediately. All route one – a Shilton goal-kick was flicked on by Harford and again by Saunders, who found Williams in space. A Southampton defender came across to tackle him, but a combination of Williams's strength and the defender's slip gave him a clear sight of goal. He could have run on with the ball but chose to shoot straight away and beat the 'keeper.

After 21 minutes Mark Wright limped out of the game to be replaced by another youngster in Jason Kavanagh, and as things turned out that was to be Wright's last appearance at the Baseball Ground, although he did play in the last game of the season at Luton Town. Kavanagh, just 19, had been voted Rams Young Player of the Year and had also played in nine First Division games, four as a substitute.

Midway through the first half, Derby doubled their lead. George Williams, inside the Derby half, was allowed time and space to look up and play a ball over the top of the Southampton defensive line who were pushing up. Southampton were playing with five defenders, and the two left-sided defenders (particularly Gittens) were out of line with the other three, and this is the area that Paul Williams ran into. Williams ran to the edge of the penalty area and, before Flowers could get too close to narrow the angle, shot into the net past the 'keeper.

Shortly afterwards, the visitors pulled a goal back when Derby's defence were caught looking for an offside when a ball was played over them from halfway. Rod Wallace, the speedy, small forward ran on and unleashed an unstoppable shot high into the helpless Shilton's goal.

Five minutes before the half-time whistle, the two-goal advantage was restored. Ted McMinn beat his marker on the left, and as defender Gittens came over to cover he just clattered into him. The referee had no hesitation in awarding the penalty-kick and gave Williams the chance to claim a first half hat-trick at the Osmaston End. He showed no nerves as he ran straight up and hit the ball left footed, high to Flowers left.

Gittens was at fault again on the hour as he tried to head the ball back, no one reacted to it except Saunders who left the defender flat footed and ran on and slipped the ball under Flowers as he came out.

At 4–1 the game was won, much to the relief of everyone involved, as it had been on 1 December since the last League win, a 2–1 win at Sunderland, which was 19 League games ago.

The scoring had not finished as there were to be a further three goals in the last five minutes of the game. Derby's free-kick five yards outside the Southampton penalty area had three Derby players over the ball, with Saunders the favourite to take a direct shot. The ball was whipped in towards Harford who, although he got to it, could not direct his header. Southampton were not able to clear the ball and it came to Justin Phillips 12 yards out, who hooked it between two defenders and past Flowers for his first senior goal in only his second game.

At the other end, a minute later, Mel Sage gave away a penalty, which Matt le Tissier coolly put to Shilton's left, to make the score 5–2. In the last minute, another Derby free-kick just outside the penalty area was floated to the back post. Tim Flowers decided to come for the ball but was unable to get to it. Mick Harford nodded it back into the centre for Saunders to head into the net, unmarked. There were three Southampton defenders on the goalline, all of them unable to stop the ball.

The 6–2 score equalled the highest score for a home game against Southampton, dating back to September 1973. Following the confirmed relegation a couple of weeks previously, this game was not a huge attraction for the fans to turn up and watch and recorded the lowest attendance for a League game during the season of just 11,680. The *News of the World* reporter wrote: 'With Wright and Saunders due to be sold, the youngsters grabbed their chance to stake a claim'.

The match programme carried a warning notice to potential fans wishing to go to the last game. Derby were to visit relegation-threatened Luton Town for the last match of the season. Luton were operating a members only admittance policy which excluded ticket sales to any away supporters. A universally unpopular move from the Bedfordshire club, they would not lift the ban even though Derby had nothing to play for; however, quite a number of Derby fans (and one suspects that fans of other clubs used similar tactics) had registered on the Luton database at the beginning of the season and were able to purchase tickets, and so several car loads were able to gain admittance.

PAUL WILLIAMS

Born: 26 March 1971

Debut v Crystal Palace (away), 20 March 1990, Division One, draw 1–1

Last game v Watford (away), 7 May 1995, Division Two, lost 1–2

First goal v Luton Town (home), 5 May 1990, Division One, lost 2–3

Bought from:

Sold to: Coventry City

Total appearances: 185 + 10 subs, 33 goals

Consecutive appearances: 35 from 16 April 1991 to 4 January 1992

Williams was born in Burton and progressed through Derby's youth-team set up, initially as a left-back and then a midfield player. He won six England Under-21 caps as his midfield displays caught the eye, and he was the club's leading scorer when they returned to Division Two in 1991–92, with 16 goals.

He also represented the Football League against an Italian Serie B team as prelude to the re-introduction of the Anglo-Italian Cup competition. By the time he left Derby he had been converted to a centre-half. He played in the 1994 Play-off Final and was responsible for Leicester's equalising goal when he misjudged the bounce and spin of the ball when trying to head it instead of kicking it clear.

With Derby unable to escape the second tier, he wanted to try his hand in the Premier League, and when Jim Smith arrived in the summer of 1995 one of the first transfers saw Williams move to Coventry City for £1 million plus Sean Flynn coming to Derby as part of the deal.

BRISTOL ROVERS 2
DERBY COUNTY 3

Division Two   **Saturday 23 November 1991**

Twerton Park, Bath

Bristol Rovers: Parkin, Alexander, Twentyman, Yates (Clark, 89), Cross, Skinner, Mehew (Stewart, 80) Reece, White, Saunders, Pounder.
Derby County: Shilton, Patterson, Forsyth (Gee, 69), G. Williams, Hayward (Kavanagh, 67), Comyn, Micklewhite, Ormondroyd, Davison, P. Williams, McMinn.
Referee: T.J. Holbrook (Walsall)
Attendance: 6,513

Four days before the match, one of the true greats in Derby's history died. Jack Stamps was the genuine 'old-fashioned centre-forward' whose goalscoring record of 100 goals in 233 League games compares very well with anyone elses. His two goals in the 1946 FA Cup Final assure him of a permanent place in the names of great Derby players.

That week also marked an important change in the ownership of the club, with local businessman Lionel Pickering making a substantial financial investment to become the majority shareholder and take the position of vice-chairman. Brian Fearn, who had taken over the club during the summer, remained as chairman and sanctioned Derby's first signings for 20 months – the first being defender Andy Comyn.

Bristol Rovers were one of those teams in the early 1990s that had vacated their original home ground and were now playing their 'home' games at Twerton Park which was the home of Bath City. It was typical of a non-League ground – an uneven pitch to play on, limited facilities and buried among a housing estate and with a small capacity.

Derby had won six out of their last eight games, while Rovers themselves were unbeaten in seven, winning two and drawing five. In the League table, Derby were comfortably in third

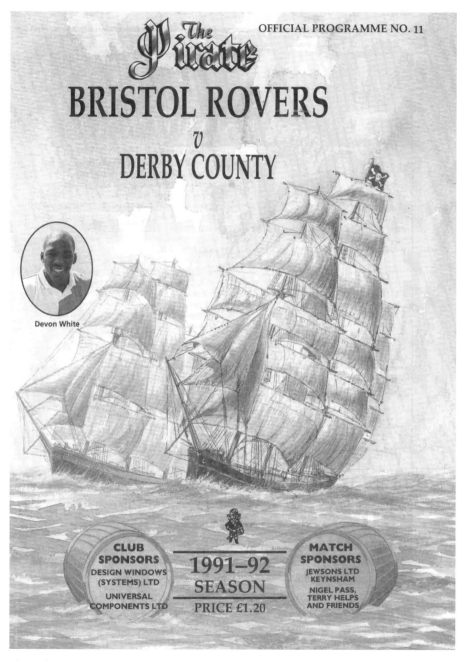

OFFICIAL PROGRAMME NO. 11

BRISTOL ROVERS
v
DERBY COUNTY

Devon White

CLUB
SPONSORS
DESIGN WINDOWS
(SYSTEMS) LTD
UNIVERSAL
COMPONENTS LTD

1991–92
SEASON
PRICE £1.20

MATCH
SPONSORS
JEWSONS LTD
KEYNSHAM
NIGEL PASS,
TERRY HELPS
AND FRIENDS

place, three points behind joint leaders Cambridge United and Middlesbrough. Bristol Rovers, despite the recent unbeaten run, found themselves third bottom, level on points with Newcastle United and a point behind Wolves.

Ted McMinn finally reached 100 appearances for Derby since signing from Seville in February 1988 and would have reached the landmark a lot sooner but for 15 months out of action with ligament problems sustained at Tottenham Hotspur in November 1989. Simon Coleman was suspended following his sending off in the recent 3–2 win at Wolves and Mel Sage was also out injured and was replaced by Mark Patterson at right-back. With Coleman missing, Michael Forsyth was moved to the centre-half position and Paul Williams moved to left-back. So it was a new defensive back line that took to the field. Bristol Rovers were unchanged for the fourth successive game and included former Derby player Steve Cross who was sold for £75,000 back in September.

It did not take long for the 1,000 Derby fans to get something to cheer, as a free-kick from Andy Comyn was initially flicked on by Patterson to Micklewhite, whose cross eventually found McMinn, who returned it into the middle of the goal for Patterson to run onto and firmly place a header into the Rovers net.

Ian Alexander became the first player to be booked when he badly fouled Ted McMinn after just 10 minutes, and as the game moved on McMinn had the pace to beat Alexander every time, and getting booked so early would hinder the defender. Not long after that, Derby old-boy Steve Cross was allowed to run through from his left-back position and shoot past Peter Shilton, although there seemed to be a valid claim for offside that was waved away.

Three minutes later, Derby found themselves 2–1 down when Paul Williams allowed a cross to get behind him and found David Mehew, who scored with a volleyed shot. Williams, drafted into the left-back position was caught out by his lack of experience in that position at this level of football.

Another consequence of the Paul Williams's move to defence was that his space in midfield was taken by Steve Hayward. Hayward struggled to make any impact on the game and was generally being by-passed, which in turn meant that George Williams was having to cover for Hayward as well. As the second half started, Derby's intentions were clear, and they pressed forward at every opportunity in search of the equaliser, without directly having a shot on target.

Hayward was eventually replaced by defender Jason Kavanagh, who slotted into the left-back position, on 67 minutes. That allowed Paul Williams to move forward into his more accustomed role.

As soon as that change happened Michael Forsyth and Devon White went for a high ball, which White won and forced a save from Shilton. Forsyth fell awkwardly injuring his upper arm/shoulder and was walked from the field by Gordon Guthrie looking like he had dislocated his shoulder.

Despite a rare attempt on the Derby goal from Carl Saunders that hit the bar, it was Derby now doing all the attacking with McMinn dominating Alexander and Gary Micklewhite going past Cross regularly.

On 80 minutes, Derby found a way back into the game as once again Micklewhite took on Steve Cross and as they raced into the penalty area, Micklewhite went down and the referee gave a penalty. Later Steve Cross said 'Gary agreed I never touched him and that he tripped but what can you do?'

Paul Williams took the penalty and scored with ease, with a well hit shot, to level the score at 2–2.

Derby finally scored the goal their possession deserved in injury time when Geoff Twentyman's back pass was a poor choice as Bobby Davison, who until that moment had made little impression on the game, collected it and rounded the Rovers goalkeeper Parkin before scoring his eighth goal in nine games. Even after the restart there were further claims for another Derby penalty as McMinn was tripped, but that would have been a bit flattering.

Another three points away from the Baseball Ground and was only the second win at a Bristol Rovers venue and took the recent points tally to 21 from a possible 27.

Overall, it was a deserved win as Derby camped around the Bristol goal for much of second half and during the game had to reorganise the defence several times after the Forsyth shoulder injury.

Late winners were becoming the norm in away games – three out of the last four had been won in the last few minutes of the game, the others being at Millwall and Wolves.

The *News of the World* commented: 'Derby remain firmly on the promotion trail, thanks to a penalty conceded by old boy Steve Cross and a giveaway goal from Geoff Twentyman' and *The People* '…they had no answer to McMinn's pace. He skinned Alexander down the left'.

Arthur Cox said 'I know that we can, individually and collectively, play better but we will certainly never show any better spirit within our team than we did on Saturday'

BOBBY DAVISON

Born: 17 July 1959
First game v Rotherham United (home), Division Two, 4 December 1982 won 3–0
Last game v Leicester City (home), Division Two, 30 November 1991, lost 1–2
First goal v Shrewsbury Town (home), Division Two, 29 December 1982, lost 2–3
Bought from: Halifax Town
Sold to: Leeds United
Total appearances: 246 + 3 subs, 106 goals
Consecutive games: 126 from 17 September 1983 to 28 December 1985

Bobby Davison first came to Derby's attention when he scored three goals against them in a League Cup tie in 1982 for Halifax Town. Within a couple of months he had been signed by Peter Taylor for £80,000.

This turned out to be a bargain fee for a true goalscorer and fans' favourite, and he was top scorer for five consecutive seasons, scoring 98 goals in his first spell at the club.

Unusually for a forward, he managed to steer clear of serious injuries and suspensions and made an impressive 126 consecutive appearances, 105 of which were League games.

On 27 November 1987 he was sold to Leeds United for a modest fee of £350,000, where he was the main striker until they signed Lee Chapman. He returned to Derby on loan in 1991 and scored eight goals in 10 games, but a permanent deal never materialised.

DERBY COUNTY 3
ASTON VILLA 4

FA Cup fourth round   Wednesday 5 February 1992

Baseball Ground

Derby County: Shilton, Kavanagh (Davidson, 84), Forsyth, G. Williams, Coleman, Comyn, Chalk (Stallard, 84), Ormondroyd, Gee, P. Williams, McMinn.
Aston Villa: Sealey, Kubicki, Small, Teale, McGrath, Richardson, Daley, Yorke, Regis, Parker, Froggatt (Carruthers, 87). Other sub: Breitkreutz.
Referee: K. Morton (Bury St Edmunds)
Attendance: 22,452

Derby and Aston Villa met on one of those famous matches at a packed Baseball Ground under the floodlights in the fourth round of the FA Cup on 5 February 1992

Both teams needed replays to progress from the third round, Villa winning 1–0 away at the Cup holders Tottenham Hotspur, while Derby had to overcome the Fourth Division leaders, Burnley, having the initial replay at the Baseball Ground abandoned 17 minutes from the end with Derby winning 2–0. One of Derby's scorers was Mark Patterson, who had suffered knee ligament damage and would not play again during the season.

The rearranged replay put back the fixture to the Saturday of the fourth round, with the winners having to play 10 days later in a mid-week fixture. Derby and Villa last met in the FA Cup in 1946 when Derby ran out 5–4 winners over the two legs.

Derby had spent £1 million a little over a week previously on the former Sunderland and Crystal Palace striker Marco Gabbiadini, and he had scored the winning goal on his debut at Portsmouth. He was Cup tied and his place was taken by Phil Gee, who Gabbiadini had been bought to replace. Derby's home form in the Second Division was not great and they had lost 6 of the 13 home games played to date. The League table had an unfamiliar look to it, Southend

THE RAM MAGAZINE

F.A. CUP FOURTH ROUND
Derby County v Aston Villa
WEDNESDAY 5 FEBRUARY 1992 · KICK-OFF 7.45

The Official Matchday Programme of Derby County FC · £1.00

Match Sponsor:
Bass Worthington

United and Cambridge United were both in the leading four teams, while Newcastle United were second bottom.

Derby's team had former Villa players Andy Comyn at the centre of defence and the tall, lanky Ian Ormondroyd up front alongside the recalled Gee. Villa, managed by Ron Atkinson and assisted by Andy Gray and physio and ex-Derby player Jim Walker, were without Steve Staunton and were suffering something of a goal drought, having scored just one goal in their previous six games. Despite that, they were still lying in sixth place in the First Division.

Derby kicked-off, playing towards the Osmaston End, packed with Villa fans who had made the short journey up the A38. After just four minutes, Derby took the lead. Ormondroyd won the ball on Derby's right and found Chalk running to the centre of the field. Ted McMinn was in space on the left hand corner of the penalty area when he was released by Chalk and ran with pace at the full-back Kubici. McMinn beat him and fired the ball goalwards. Whether this was an attempt at a cross or meant as a shot is unclear, but Les Sealey in the goal could not hold the ball and it bounced up very nicely for Phil Gee to nod the ball into the net from a yard out, his third goal of the season. The immediate feeling of elation in the crowd was dampened when they realised there was still another 86 minutes to play.

The fans' fears were realised just four minutes after taking the lead when Simon Coleman had to make a covering tackle on Dwight Yorke. The resulting corner was taken by Kevin Richardson from the Popside corner. The whipped-in corner evaded Ormondroyd, but was flicked on by McGrath at the near post, more upwards than flat with pace towards the back post. Three Derby defenders jumped for the ball with Cyrille Regis, and the ball fell in the centre of the six yard area to Yorke and he stabbed the ball straight at Peter Shilton on the goalline. The goalkeeper was unable to react quick enough and, despite the efforts of Kavanagh, the ball bobbled into the corner of the net for Yorke's 12th goal of the season.

The game had changed dramatically by the mid-point of the first-half, with Villa scoring two more goals in a four-minute spell, which should have sealed the game. The first one, that gave Villa the lead for the first time, was again a goalmouth scramble. Shilton had saved well, pushing the ball away, when a Tony Daley shot from the right hand corner of the area was driven goalwards. The corner bypassed everyone and Shilton, under no pressure, instead of catching the ball, tipped it over the bar for another corner to be taken from the opposite side. This time Froggatt took the corner and the 'keeper came and jumped up with two Villa forwards to claim the ball. He never really had a clean hold of the ball, and as he hit the ground the ball spilt out and bounced nicely for Yorke, again in the middle of the six-yard box. He reacted first and hit the ball more into the ground than directly hard into the goal. Three defenders were between him and the goal and were caught flat-footed as the ball bounced agonisingly over all of them into the corner of the net.

Shilton and the defenders chased the referee appealing for a free-kick for a possible foul on the goalkeeper, but referee Morton seemed happy that he had dropped the ball.

Four minutes later, the tie seemed to be over. Chalk lost possession on the halfway line allowing Garry Parker (a £650,000 buy from Nottingham Forest the previous November) to run unchallenged through the centre. Derby defenders were backing off all the while, keeping an eye on Yorke, in particular, and inevitably inviting a shot on goal. Parker duly obliged by hitting an unstoppable shot from outside of the penalty area into the top corner of Shilton's goal – the goalkeeper, who would have seen the run and shot from a long way out didn't move on his goalline.

From being a goal up after four minutes, they now found themselves 3–1 down some 20 minutes later, although that scoreline did not reflect how evenly matched the two teams were. Ted McMinn on Derby's left was always a handful for the Villa defence and he was the most likely to create more chances to get Derby back into the game, especially playing in front of a packed 'C' Stand.

On 38 minutes, that is exactly what happened – George Williams won the ball in the middle of the Villa half and fed the ball to the waiting McMinn. He drew out McGrath from the centre, turned him one way then the other before chipping the ball over. With McGrath out of position, Ormondroyd drew the other central defender out to the edge of the six-yard box, leaving Phil Gee six yards from goal and centrally placed. With Sealey stood in the centre of the goal, a header placed either side would certainly score. Gee, a Villa fan himself, placed it to Sealey's right and his dive did not get close.

Hopes of a revival were dashed a minute later as a long clearance was flicked on by Regis, who out-jumped Comyn and left Coleman and Yorke in a race for the ball. As they chased the ball into the area, Yorke got ahead of the defender and appeared to be pulled back as they both fell over. Possibly Shilton could have come out and smothered the ball to avert any danger early on. The referee had no doubts and pointed to the penalty spot, although Coleman thought that he had been fouled by the forward earlier in the move. Yorke took the penalty himself and placed it to Shilton's left. Shilton was not known for his penalty-saving ability and this one was not hit hard enough, placed well enough, or high enough, and he managed to keep the ball out. Unfortunately, the ball rolled back to Yorke who had an empty net to score his third and Villa's fourth goal of the game.

That brought an end to an eventful first half – six goals, a penalty saved and a hat-trick – Derby had it all to do to get anything out of the game.

McMinn was having lots of success down the left hand side of midfield, and Derby's main aim during the second half must have been to give him as much of the ball as possible. Phil Gee had a further opportunity when McMinn found Paul Williams on the edge of the penalty area and fired over a good, low cross. Gee arrived at speed with his marker and connected well but was unable to keep his shot down. Any shot on target would have given the goalkeeper no chance.

On 55 minutes, Villa had a golden opportunity to further extend their lead – a quickly taken free-kick by Richardson was played into the penalty area and as Coleman and Yorke ran towards the ball, the Derby defender was deemed to have controlled the ball with his upper arm and the referee was perfectly placed to make the judgement.

Yorke, not worried by the fact he had missed one in the first half, stepped up again. This time he put the ball to Shilton's right hand side, again low and placed for the corner. Once again the shot was not far enough into the corner and this time Shilton was able to hold on to the ball. There cannot have been many games in the 1,000-odd in which the 42-year-old Shilton played where he saved two penalties in the same game.

Derby were now throwing everything at Villa and deservedly got another goal back – the best of the game. A free-kick was awarded for a foul on Ormondroyd in front of the Derby dug out and was quickly taken to Chalk on the right wing. His cross was played to the penalty spot and found Paul Williams falling backwards and in mid-air, who launched an unstoppable volley that Sealey could not get near.

Chances were coming at both ends as the game opened up further, Regis headed a decent chance wide after Forsyth slipped and gave him a free header, and they came even closer 15 minutes from the end as a throw in by Jason Kavanagh, deep in the Derby half, was not properly cleared and Tony Daley ran into the penalty area and unleashed a thunderous shot which hit the outside of the post and went out for a goal-kick.

McMinn was still seeing plenty of the ball and on 80 minutes, on halfway, cut inside his marker and was stopped in his tracks by a blatant obstruction offence. Polish international, Kubici had already been booked in the first half which left the referee little option but to issue a red card.

Paul Williams found himself centrally placed on the edge of the penalty area, back to goal. A quick turn to his right and a shot with his left foot on the turn was heading towards goal. Sealy dived and was able to catch the ball in mid-air to make a fine, spectacular save. A few more inches higher or wider and it was a certain goal.

A double substitution saw the introduction of young Mark Stallard into the attack for his sixth appearance for the club, replacing Martyn Chalk and Jonathan Davidson replacing Kavanagh at right-back. Stalllard's first piece of the action was to send over a cross from the left wing in the area where Villa were down to 10 men. His deep cross was met by Gee, who placed his header back across goal and, with Sealy flat footed and beaten, the ball scraped the outside of the post and bounced wide.

Tony Daley was now filling in at right-back and Villa withdrew all their players behind the ball trying to see out time. As the time moved into the 93rd minute, Forsyth swung over a cross that beat Sealey and bounced on top of the crossbar. At that the referee blew the final whistle and Villa had scraped through and Derby could feel unlucky not to have earned at least a replay from the game. Both sets of fans applauded the players from the field.

Alan Hansen, on the BBC *Sportsnight* programme, said that 'you would struggle to see a better game all season' and 'it was a shame Derby had to go out as they had contributed enormously to the game'.

The winners, Aston Villa, had a fifth-round tie away to Swindon Town to look forward to, which they won 2–1 and then were knocked out in the following round in yet another away game, this time at the eventual Cup winners, Liverpool.

There was a growing feeling that Shilton was past his best, to a large extent confirmed to all during this game. By the end of the month there were major changes to the Derby team; Peter Shilton had played his last game for Derby and had left to become manager at Plymouth Argyle leaving his understudy, Martin Taylor, to take over until the experienced Steve Sutton was signed for £300,000 from Nottingham Forest. Paul Kitson also arrived from Leicester City, with Gee and Ormondroyd going the other way

Despite the classic British football match played out between the two teams, Arthur Cox, examining the match, said it was 'disrespectful defending allied to wasteful finishing which led to Aston Villa coming out on top'.

Phil Gee said it was a 'marvellous Cup tie...one of the quickest games that I've ever played in'.

The attendance of 22,452 generated record receipts for a Derby County game of £150,000.

PHIL GEE

Born: 19 December 1964
Debut v Brentford (away), Freight-Rover Trophy 15 January 1986, draw 0–0
Last game v Bristol Rovers (home), Division Two 15 February 1992, won 1–0
First goal v Rotherham United, Division Three, 9 May 1986 won 2–1
Bought from: Gresley Rovers
Sold to: Leicester City
Total appearances: 131 + 21 subs, 31 goals
Consecutive appearances: 60 from 3 September 1986 to 10 October 1987

A painter and decorator by trade, Gee was scoring lots of goals for Riley Sports and then briefly for Gresley Rovers at non-League level.

Former Derby favourite David Nish was chairman at Gresley at that time and recommended Gee after only a few games in a short two-month stay and eventually received £5,000 from Derby based on his appearances. His direct running and shooting saw him notch up an impressive 31 goals in 28 games in the Central League in his first season, 1985–86. His first-team debut came in the Freight-Rover Trophy at Brentford in January 1986.

He made his League debut in the 3–1 home win against his home-town club, Walsall on 12 March, and he also came on as a substitute in the crucial Division Three match against Rotherham United on a wet Friday night, and scored the first goal with a

direct run from halfway before coolly finishing. He scored 15 goals in Derby's Division Two Championship season, but things got a lot harder in the top division against international and vastly more experienced defenders. He still managed to finish joint top scorer with John Gregory on six goals in that first season in the top League.

Derby needed more firepower to survive at the top level, and Gee was replaced by the likes of Paul Goddard, Dean Saunders, Marco Gabbiadini and Mick Harford. He went on a run of 13 games without a goal in the 1991–92 season, and his last goals were in the 4–3 FA Cup defeat to Aston Villa in February 1992.

He was sold, along with Ian Ormondroyd, to Leicester City as part of the deal that brought Paul Kitson to Derby during Arthur Cox's and Lionel Pickering's reshaping of the team.

DERBY COUNTY 1 WOLVERHAMPTON WANDERERS 2

Division Two   **Saturday 21 March 1992**

Baseball Ground

Derby County: Taylor, Kavanagh, Forsyth, G. Williams, Coleman, Comyn, Johnson, Kitson, Gabbiadini, P. Williams, Simpson (McMinn, 82). Other sub: Micklewhite.
Wolverhampton Wanderers: Stowell, Ashley (Downing, 69), Venus, Bennett, Rankine, Madden, Birch, Cook, Bull, Mutch, Burke. Other sub: Simkin.
Referee: M.L. James (Horsham)
Attendance: 21,024

This game was the nearest home game to the 100th anniversary of the first game played by Derby County at the Baseball Ground, which was 19 March 1892 when they were beaten 0–1 by Sunderland.

This was only a temporary move as the Racecourse was still their official home pitch, but the football club had to bow to the wishes of their landlords who wanted to stage a race meeting on the same day that the Sunderland game was scheduled. Sir Francis Ley came to their rescue and offered them the use of his sports ground, from where he ran a very successful baseball team.

The match programme for the game was increased by an additional 16 pages that was related to the Baseball Ground and its personalities from the previous 100 years. Every supporter attending the game was given a voucher that they could redeem for a personalised certificate showing they were present at this centenary game.

Derby kept the same team that had lost the previous week at Tranmere Rovers, 3–4 after being in front at one stage by 3–1, where a number of players made individual mistakes that cost the game. This was, however, the only defeat in the previous six games and Derby began the day in seventh place. Their home form was the big disappointment of the season (losing seven of the 17 home games so far) and the biggest factor in them not challenging for a position in the automatic promotion places. The home form had improved greatly, winning the last three home games after going some three months without one earlier in the season. As a contrast, the away form was the third best in the division.

Wolves were in 11th place, some seven points further behind. Derby were rebuilding quickly, and the new team was taking shape thanks to Mr Pickering's personal wealth, with Tommy Johnson making his debut the previous week and set for his home debut. Paul Kitson had joined 11 days prior to the game from Leicester City who took Phil Gee and Ian Ormondroyd in part exchange. This brought Arthur Cox's spending to nearly £4 million in six weeks on the new-look forward line of Marco Gabbiadini, Kitson, Johnson and Paul Simpson.

The biggest League gate of the season so far of 21,024 attended, encouraged by the recent good home form and to get a look at the new expensive team that Arthur Cox was putting together. The strong wind blowing in and around the Baseball Ground would have made Wolves wish that Derek Mountfield was playing, but a bout of flu kept him out.

Paul Kitson, eager to make a good impression for the home fans, had two opportunities for Derby early on. A cross from Paul Williams was probably overhit as although Kitson got to the ball with his head, the angle was far too tight to make a serious attempt at goal. His second chance came from a Gabbiadini pass, and it was a disappointing finish.

The opening goal came in first-half injury time. A corner by Paul Simpson was only partially cleared to the edge of the area, where a Tommy Johnson shot could only be parried by Mike Stowell who would have seen it late coming through a group of players.

Paul Kitson followed up to score his second goal, and first at the Baseball Ground, for Derby in his third appearance. Kitson was unlucky not to score again in the second half, when again Gabbiadini was the provider and his low shot was only partially stopped by Stowell and the ball continued on its path to goal. Bennet, who was Mountfield's replacement, raced back and just managed to clear the ball before Gabbiadini could force it over the line.

At 2–0, Wolves would have no chance, based on what we had seen so far of forcing their way back into the game as their main style of play was a long ball, influenced by the strong wind, towards Steve Bull. Simon Coleman and Andy Comyn were coping well with everything so far.

With 17 minutes remaining Derby were still leading through Paul Kitson's goal, but things changed dramatically. Michael Forsyth blocked a shot on the edge of the Derby area but ended up on the floor and inadvertently touched the ball with a hand. Referee Mike James awarded a penalty although it was hardly deliberate and probably should not have been given. Paul Birch stepped up after a delay and scored with ease to pull Wolves level.

Straight from the kick-off, Wolves scored again in a move that was gifted to them by a set of individual errors starting with George Williams, who until then had been controlling the game. He was badly caught in possession by Andy Mutch who from a left wing position hit a long,, hopeful centre. After keeping a tight reign on Steve Bull all afternoon with relative ease, Simon Coleman lost concentration and gave him far too much time and space, and although he could only just get a slight touch to the ball it proved to be enough to score his 20th goal of the season.

Martin Taylor mis-judged it completely and dived too early as the ball bounced agonisingly over him into the net. Hindsight is a wonderful thing, but if Taylor had stayed in his goal and not dived the ball would have come to him with little pace on it and he could have made a routine save. That goal for Bull took him to number 195 for Wolves and made him the club's leading all-time scorer, beating John Richards (who had a 10-game loan spell with Derby in 1982).

From Derby's point of view the only thing missing was a second goal as they had dominated the possession and had the majority of the chances in the game; however, in the space of 60 seconds they had gone from 1–0 up and in total control of the game, playing good football and creating chances to 1–2 down.

As usual, Arthur Cox was not willing to publically single out players for criticism but made some general comments afterwards; 'The penalty and goal from the kick-off affected everyone – left everyone frustrated, doubting and annoyed that three points has slipped away.

'The penalty was one of those 50:50 decisions – the second was down to lack of concentration by a number of players leading to Steve Bull scoring the winner.

'We created many chances with good, accurate football and have only ourselves to blame for not winning the game comfortably.'

Martin Taylor seemed to take the blame for the Tranmere and Wolves defeats and was replaced in goals by Steve Sutton for the rest of the season.

Blackburn and Leicester lost at home (to Charlton and Watford respectively) and Portsmouth went down at Oxford United and Cambridge United were drawing with Ipswich Town – it was a major chance missed to narrow the gap. Defeat saw The Rams drop two places in the table and now desperately needed to beat a struggling Plymouth

Argyle team the following Wednesday in a re-arranged home game after the original was postponed in December. They won this game comfortably 2–0.

PAUL KITSON

Born: 9 January 1971

Debut v Port Vale (home), 11 March 1992, Division Two, won 3–1

Last Game v Oldham Athletic (home), 17 September 1994, Division One, won 2–1

First Goal v Tranmere Rovers (away), 14 March 1992, Division Two, lost 3–4

Bought from: Leicester City

Sold to: Newcastle United

Total appearances: 130 + 1 subs, 49 goals

Consecutive games: 34 from 14 November 1992 to 2 April 1993

Leicester City received a club-record £1.3 million for his transfer fee in March 1992, which was made up of £800,000 and Phil Gee and Ian Ormondroyd moving to Leicester in part-exchange. Arthur Cox described him as having '...all the qualities to develop into an outstanding player'.

Kitson's first full season with Derby saw him score 17 goals in 44 League games and another 13 the following as Derby failed to get promotion, losing the Play-off Final against his old club, although he was only a substitute.

Eight games into the 1994–95 season, Newcastle United made an offer of £2,250,000, which was initially turned down by the Derby chairman Lionel Pickering who felt that Kitson was worth between £3 to £4 million. However, Pickering was outvoted 1–4 by the club's directors and reluctantly agreed to the transfer, which went ahead on 24 September.

After an initial successful period, the arrival of established strikers of the calibre of Les Ferdinand and Faustino Asprilla meant Kitson was only a squad player. He was knocked further down the list by the arrival of Alan Shearer and left in February 1997 to join West Ham United, just weeks after the resignation of manager Kevin Keegan.

BLACKBURN ROVERS 4
DERBY COUNTY 2

Division Two Play-off semi-final, first leg   **Sunday 10 May 1992**

Ewood Park

Blackburn Rovers: Mimms, May, Wright, Cowans, Moran (Richardson, 56), Hendry, Price, Atkins, Speedie (Shearer, 71), Newell, Sellars.
Derby County: Sutton, Kavanagh, Forsyth, McMinn (Ramage, 71), Coleman, Comyn, Johnson, Kitson, Gabbiadini (Micklewhite, 71), P. Williams, Simpson.
Referee: K.S. Hackett (Sheffield)
Attendance: 19,677

The regular season had finished with Derby in third place on 78 points, two points behind Middlesbrough who occupied the second automatic promotion place. Blackburn finished sixth and so had to play at home in the first leg. The other Play-off semi-final was between Leicester City and Cambridge United.

Derby had, in fact, been just 13 minutes from securing the automatic promotion place to the Premier League on the last day of the regular season – they were beating Swindon Town at home, while Leicester were losing at home to a relegation-threatened Newcastle United and Middlesbrough drawing at Wolverhampton Wanderers and being reduced to 10 men. Paul Wilkinson's 24th goal of the season on 77 minutes meant that Derby could not overtake them and Wolves were not able to force an equaliser. The use of the radio among fans kept everyone up to date with events elsewhere, and Derby then had to settle for a Play-off place.

Blackburn clinched a place in the top six by winning 3–1, thanks to a David Speedie hat-trick on the last day of the season and consigning Peter Shilton's Plymouth Argyle to the Third Division. Blackburn had been three points clear at the top on 14 March, but six straight defeats in the next month had seen them drop out of the top six. Blackburn had stunned the football world in October 1990

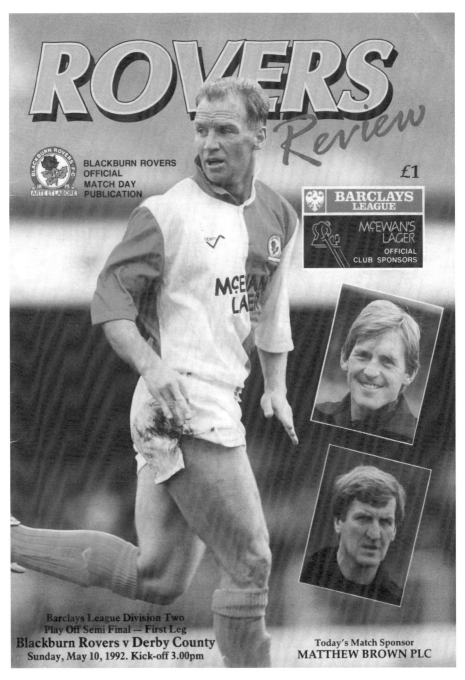

BLACKBURN ROVERS
OFFICIAL
MATCH DAY
PUBLICATION

£1

BARCLAYS
LEAGUE

MCEWAN'S
LAGER

OFFICIAL
CLUB SPONSORS

Barclays League Division Two
Play Off Semi Final — First Leg
Blackburn Rovers v Derby County
Sunday, May 10, 1992. Kick-off 3.00pm

Today's Match Sponsor
MATTHEW BROWN PLC

when Kenny Dalglish, who had previously resigned from the Liverpool manager post, moved to Blackburn, heavily backed by millionaire Jack Walker, and they had added Roy Wegerle to their forward line for £1.5 million in March, as well as Mike Newell (£1.2 million from Everton) and Duncan Shearer (£750,000 from Swindon Town).

The first leg was at Ewood Park, with Derby in fine form, winning their last four games and six out of the last eight, drawing the other two.

Paul Williams had recovered from his back injury that kept him out of the Swindon victory, but captain Geraint Williams was not yet fit enough to be considered for a place for either leg of the semi-finals, despite having been at Lilleshall all week having treatment on his knee. Ted McMinn, named Player of the Year, had been a revelation in the centre of midfield and was preferred to the improving Craig Ramage. McMinn had been playing in central midfield for several weeks, instead of his usual wing position.

The pitch condition was not good. Having endured a heavy winter, it was now May and the pitch had dried out and parts of the turf had been worn away, meaning that the ball could run unevenly and bounce erratically.

Everyone connected with Derby could not have wished for a better start. After just three minutes, Paul Kitson ran onto a ball played forward by Paul Williams and was fouled by Colin Hendry. The other Paul – Simpson – took the free-kick and whipped in one of the crosses he was renowned for and Marco Gabbiadini found space and dived in to head the ball past Bobby Mimms.

Within a quarter of an hour Derby had added a second goal, started by McMinn in the middle of the field. His central-midfield colleague received a pass and played the ball towards Simpson on the left wing. Simpson knocked the ball through the middle, and Tommy Johnson put the ball past Mimms. It was 2–0 to Derby and thoughts were turning towards Wembley, and now should have been the time for an old head in the centre of midfield to calm everyone down and keep things tight for the next half hour. Cox and McFarland could not have planned this start better if they had tried.

Blackburn, despite the scoreline, were already making chances of their own. Speedie missed an opportunity, Sellars hit the outside of a post and Hendry had a couple of shots saved by Steve Sutton, and these should have been warning signs to the Derby midfield and defence.

Derby's style of play had changed from being quick and one-touch play through the midfield to holding the ball for too long and making wrong decisions when they passed the ball. It was unfortunate that Geraint Williams was not risked, as his midfield harrying and tackles may have made an important difference in this important first leg. The inexperience of McMinn in the central midfield role and Williams fitness may have contributed, but neither of them were able to stop the Blackburn players running through them almost at will, and this meant that the defence came under constant pressure and sooner rather than later this would result in a goal for them.

A stroke of luck for Blackburn on 35 minutes was the turning point in the game. Simpson fouled David Speedie a couple of yards outside the area. Sellars took the free-kick but did not connect with it as he would have liked. Paul Williams was jumping and turning in the wall and deflected the weak shot. That left Sutton hopelessly wrong-footed and, ever so slowly, the ball trundled over the line.

Buoyed by that goal, Blackburn continued to press and just before half-time they managed an equaliser that came about because of poor defending. Gordon Cowans passed out to the left and Mike Newell came inside Comyn and brushed aside a tame challenge from Williams. From 25 yards out, the way to goal opened and he unleased a shot that Steve Sutton could do nothing about.

Derby's attacking force was rarely seen in this passage of play and there was just one of note – Kitson should have done better when the McMinn/Johnson combination set up an opportunity, but Kitson's chip was the wrong choice of shot from such a promising position.

It was still Blackburn that were creating the better and more frequent chances – Newell had a goal ruled out for offside and Hendry had a header cleared off the line. On 65 minutes Blackburn took the lead for the first time in the tie – another individual defensive mistake, this time by Andy Comyn, allowed Atkins to thread a pass for Speedie to score easily. Derby's defence were shaken and looked likely to concede at every Blackburn attack.

At this stage, Derby would have taken the result and taken time to re-organise and plot a 1–0 win in the return leg. Within five minutes, the scoreline got even worse with a simple, route one goal. A Mimms clearance was headed on by Newell and Speedie scored – very easy and distressing for Derby's management with the ease in which they were being cut open so regularly. McMinn and Gabbiadini were substituted, but it could easily have been Paul Williams as he was clearly off the pace and failed to stop the Blackburn midfield from passing and moving around him.

Blackburn sat back a little and allowed Derby to get back into the game in the last 15 minutes without creating a clear chance.

Afterwards, the Derby manager said – 'we were alive, confident, tactically excellent and took a two-goal lead and for the first 30 minutes we most certainly held the upper hand...we lost the respect for the opposition in those crucial 10 minutes before half-time and conceded two very poor goals...we now know fully exactly the magnitude of the task ahead of us. We know the time period. We know the scorelines. We know the opposition. There is a still a tremendous amount of football to be played before this tie is settled' – more in optimism than belief.

All this was in vain as, although Derby won the second leg 2–1, this meant that it was Blackburn who won the tie 5–4 on aggregate and went on to play, and beat, Leicester City 1–0 in the Final at Wembley to join the new Premier League.

The rules of the Play-offs have changed over the years, but in 1991 away goals did count double in the event of level score at the end of 30 minutes extra time at the end of the second leg. So a 2–0 win for Derby would have been enough.

This was Gary Micklewhite's last appearance for Derby – his family wanting a return back down south, closer to their families. He was the longest-serving player on the staff, having been signed in 1985 from Queen's Park Rangers.

MARCO GABBIADINI

Born: 20 January 1968

Debut v Portsmouth (away), Division Two, 1 February 1992, won 1–0

Last game v Middlesbrough (home), FA Cup, 8 March 1997, lost 0–2

First goal v Portsmouth (away), Division Two, 1 February 1992, won 1–0

Bought from: Crystal Palace

Sold to: Panionios, Greece

Total appearances: 200 + 27 subs, 68 goals

Consecutive appearances: 52 from 29 August 1992 to 2 April 1993

Gabbiadini started his career at York City and followed his manager, Denis Smith, to Sunderland for a fee of £80,000. He soon became a key player for Sunderland, who were then a Third Division team, scoring goals on a regular basis and becoming a fans favourite. Sunderland's rise through the divisions brought national attention and a call up to the England B squad. Ian Wright's move to Arsenal prompted Crystal Palace to pay £1.8 million for him at the start of the 1991–92 season

After just four months, he failed to settle in the South despite scoring seven goals in 25 games and was transferred to Derby for £1 million as part of Arthur Cox's spending spree funded by Lionel Pickering.

He scored the only goal of the game on his debut at Portsmouth in February 1992, and at the end of his first full season he was voted the Player of the Year. A year later, he scored Derby's only goal in the Anglo-Italian Cup Final at Wembley. He was an integral part of the team that eventually won promotion to the Premier League in 1995–96.

The emergence of Paulo Wanchope, Baiano, Burton, Sturridge meant that opportunities were becoming limited for Gabbiadini, and he accepted an offer to move to Greek side Panionios. He went on to make over 750 appearances in total, also playing for Birmingham City, Oxford United, Stoke City, Darlington, Northampton Town and Hartlepool United before being forced to retire in 2004 following a series of knee injuries.

DERBY COUNTY 3
BRISTOL CITY 4

Division One   **Sunday 6 September 1992**

Baseball Ground

Derby County: Sutton, Kavanagh, Forsyth, Pembridge, Coleman, Wassall, Gabbiadini (Micklewhite, 52), Kitson, Johnson (Comyn, 78), Williams, Simpson.
Bristol City: Welch, Mitchell, Scott, Thompson, Bryant, Osman, Mellon, Dziekanowski, Allison, Harrison (Bent, 45), Shelton. Other sub: Edwards.
Referee: P. W. Harrison (Heywood)
Attendance: 12,738

Derby came into this match sitting bottom of the newly formed First Division (this was the first season of the Premier League) having failed to win any of their first four League games, which was not an ideal start by the bookies pre-season favourites for the title.

Derby's only success so far was in the previous Wednesday night's 4–2 win over Notts County in the preliminary round of the Anglo-Italian Cup. Ted McMinn was missing because of a knee injury, but welcomed back Marco Gabbiadini into the starting line up. Bristol City had a problem with their forward line with first-choice strikers Leroy Rosenior and Andrew Cole (who already had scored five goals since his summer transfer from Arsenal) both out injured and left them with just Wayne Allison to choose from, forcing them into a 5–4–1 type formation.

The feeling before the game was that Bristol had come to get a point or limit the number of goals that Derby would score against them, being marshalled at the back by former Repton pupil and current assistant manager Russell Osman. With Derby's forwards always likely to cause problems for any opposition defence, a repeat of the previous season's 4–1 scoreline looked a likely good bet. Bristol City were still unbeaten in the early stages of the season.

On a bright and sunny afternoon, Derby kicked-off towards the Osmaston End in front of the ITV live cameras. After some early pressure, Derby's first attempt on goal was from a corner that came over to Tommy Johnson, whose header was downwards and was cleared at the foot of the post. The early pressure by the home team paid off in the 11th minute following a passage of scrappy play in midfield that eventually forced

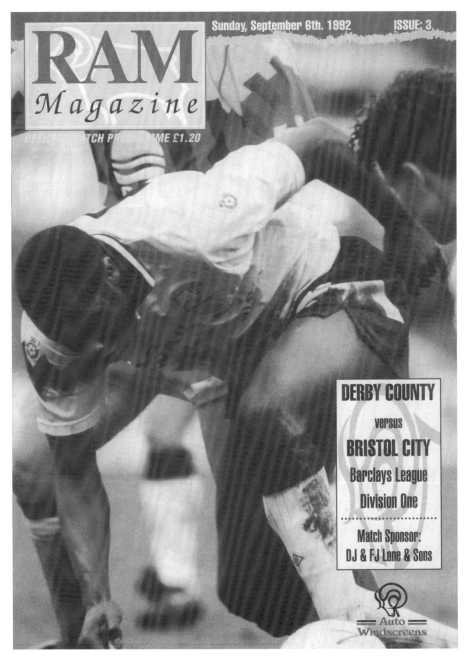

the Bristol left-back Scott into an error when trying to find his own player in the centre circle. Paul Williams made a telling interception and ran a further 20 yards before passing to Paul Simpson on the left wing. The right-back was nowhere to be seen, allowing Simpson to run into the penalty area, and he took one touch and slotted the ball under the 'keeper for his fourth goal of the season.

Within two minutes, the lead had been doubled. It was a classic goal, from one end of the field to the other in three passes. Williams cleared the ball from inside the Derby penalty area to half-way where Gabbiadini helped it on to Kitson who was 30 yards out with back to goal and marked by Osman. A superb reverse pass put Simpson in again from an identical position to his first goal, and again the right-back was hopelessly out of position. This time, as the 'keeper advanced, Simpson just lifted the ball over him and into the net.

Every time Derby got the ball forward, the pace and movement of Kitson, Johnson and Gabbiadini, as predicted, was causing all sorts of problems for the Bristol defence who had not quite settled into the 5–4–1 formation.

Derby continued to press forward and created a chance for Simon Coleman this time. Kitson robbed Scott on the edge of the City penalty area and whipped over a cross which was met by Coleman. Anything on target would have gone in, but he was unable to keep the ball down.

The Robins were limited to long balls forward to the lone striker, but he was largely alone and the midfield and full-backs were not getting forward in the right positions at the right time to provide any real threat to the Derby defence.

The third goal in any game is crucial – 3–0 and the game should be over, 2–1 and the game is suddenly back alive with the impetus with side just scoring. Paul Simpson should have wrapped the game up for Derby on the 28th minute. Another Bristol City attack ended harmlessly and allowed Steve Sutton to kick out quickly. The defender mis-judged the ball as it bounced over him and released Kitson in space. Osman came over as the covering defender to block Kitson, leaving Gabbiadini free in the middle. Kitson played the ball behind Gabbiadini and found Simpson in the same position that brought him two goals already. This time his hard, low shot hit the goalkeeper's legs and bounced away for a throw. At 3–0, that would have been game over and ensured Derby's first win of the season.

The game turned on its head on 35 minutes. An innocuous City attack was put out for a throw, in front of the 'A' Stand. The resulting long throw was initially flicked on by the centre-half Thompson and caused all sorts of panic in the home defence as it fell to Allison and Shelton. Neither of them could get a firm touch on the ball as Sutton came out to claim it. The ball broke free and seemed as though it was going to roll over the line or Shelton, following up, would tap it in. Sutton, however, inexplicably rugby tackled Shelton two yards out, and Forsyth booted the ball off the line. The referee had no option but to give the penalty and to send off the Derby 'keeper, who was a week away from his testimonial match against Nottingham Forest at the City Ground.

Paul Williams was handed the gloves to take over in goal, and his first job was to pick the ball out of the net as Martin Scott, who had had a torrid time in the game so far, calmly slotted the ball into Williams's left hand corner of the net. Williams later joked 'I stepped up for the penalty because it didn't look like anybody else wanted the job'.

The rules in the Premier League were different at this time, allowing a substitute goalkeeper to be named and brought on in such circumstances (as Sheffield United did in a recent fixture in the top division). The rules in the Football League did not allow this and clubs were limited to the two substitutes.

There were a number of bad tackles on Derby players before the half-time break – firstly Mellon brought down Pembridge with a scything tackle and as the ball broke loose Thompson clattered into Gabbiadini. Mellon went into the referees notebook for his challenge.

Five minutes before the interval, Gabbiadini, back to goal on the edge of the penalty area was brought down with the linesman flagging furiously. After a lengthy debate among the officials, the referee booked Thompson with a suspicion of stamping on Gabbiadini as he was on the floor. A lucky escape for the defender as he was involved in the Mellon incident earlier.

At half-time the score was 2–1 to Derby, but with the goalkeeper off the field and down to 10 men. The team talks by the managers would be very different –Arthur Cox had to try and get his defenders to push out and stop the Bristol players from taking shots at the stand-in 'keeper and at the same time be prepared to break quickly and take advantage of Bristol having to attack to get anything from the game.

Dennis Smith, had to try and take advantage of the extra player and get more pressure on the Derby defence. To try and expose the defence, Harrison was withdrawn at half-time and young, speedy winger Junior Bent was brought on in his place.

Williams was half expecting a half-time reshuffle to allow him to return to his normal position, 'but the boss just said to continue as we were, so I was stuck with the job'.

The early pressure in the second half, as expected, was by Bristol, limiting Derby to occasional breaks forward. Derby were forced into their first substitution in the 53rd minute when Gabbiadini picked up an injury and was replaced by Gary Micklewhite, who went to his usual position on the right side of midfield, while Tommy Johnson moved into a central attacking position.

Just before the hour mark, Bristol should have equalised. Bent broke free between Forsyth and Wassall and fired in a shot that was beaten away by Williams. The ball fell to Scott whose shot hit Williams's legs, although Wassall was covering behind him on the line. Paul Williams was getting cheered every time he touched the ball and also growing in confidence and seemed to be enjoying the experience.

On 65 minutes, Mark Pembridge had the opportunity to extend the lead and possibly put the game beyond the visitors. A one-two pass with Tommy Johnson broke nicely and set Pembridge free to run into the penalty area. Welch, in the Bristol goal, came out well and blocked the attempted clip over him, although he may have been better trying to take the ball round him.

Two minutes later the visitors thought they were level. Allison, out on the left wing, made space for Scott to run into, and his shot took a deflection off Williams and fell to Bent two yards out to push into the net. The linesman in front of the Bristol fans on the away terracing flagged for offside.

Bristol eventually got an equaliser, although in fortunate circumstances. A long clearance from Osman at the back reached Thompson, who was now playing in a forward position with Derby having to play with just Johnson and Kitson up front. He had players free to his left but ignored them and his long-range shot took a wicked deflection off Kavanagh and fell into the path of Bent who was goalside of Wassall and knocked the ball under Williams before anyone could react.

With the score now at 2–2, Derby would be looking to keep things tight at the back and keep the point. With this in mind, Tommy Johnson was replaced by defender Andy Comyn, leaving Paul Kitson up front on his own. Within a matter of seconds, Bristol had scored again. The free-kick that was given that allowed the substitution to take place was played to the edge of the Derby area where Coleman missed it and the ball bounced up. Comyn followed Allison to the ball, and under pressure he headed the ball into his own net.

With 10 minutes to play and with both substitutes on the field in place of two of the recognised forwards and now a goal down, the feeling of the home crowd was that it was going to be difficult to get back into the game. But that is exactly what they did, almost immediately. Derby won a free-kick on their right wing, deep in the Bristol half. The quickly taken kick found Simpson, who had beaten the offside trap, all alone in the centre of the goal with just the 'keeper to beat. This time, he brought the ball down, took it round the 'keeper and duly completed his hat-trick. We were now back to 3–3, and a point each would have been a fair result.

With just three minutes left, a deep cross from the industrious Polish player Dziekanowski found Allison's head as he beat Forsyth to the ball. His tremendous header left Williams rooted to his line as the ball nestled right in the corner. That header would have beaten many better goalkeepers than Williams. From 2–0 down and looking a very poor side, Bristol were now leading 4–3 and could have had another as Bent was clean through but his shot was well stopped by Williams.

In the last minute another controversial decision could have changed the final result. A long ball out of defence by Forsyth found the Bristol 'keeper well out of his area and there was more than a suspicion of deliberate hand-ball that was not punished by the referee, and as the ball broke to Simpson he was unable to get enough pace on his chip shot as the 'keeper retreated back to his goal with some urgency.

In the end, Williams could not be faulted directly for any of the goals he conceded, as the sending off of Steve Sutton changed the course of the game, as it inevitably would. Arthur Cox was disappointed with the result and put it down to some inexperience in the young team as to how to play with 10 men and defend the lead from that position.

Derby had to wait a further three League games before chalking up their first League win of the season – a 2–0 home success over Southend United.

STEVE SUTTON

Born: 16 April 1961
Debut v Rotherham United (home), Division Three, 2 March 1985, draw 1–1
Last game v Sheffield United (away), Division One, 7 October 1995, won 2–0
Bought from: Nottingham Forest

Sold to: Birmingham City

Total appearances: Loan spell 14

Permanent: 81 + 1 sub

Consecutive games 23 from 16 October 1994 to 21 February 1995

Steve Sutton was brought in on loan from Nottingham Forest by Arthur Cox during the Centenary season of 1984–85 season when first-choice goalkeeper, Eric Steele, was injured. Sutton performed well during his 14 games, but finances were still tight following the High Court appearance and Derby were not able to afford the transfer fee for him at that time. He went back to Nottingham Forest and won several trophies as first-choice 'keeper.

Sutton eventually joined for a fee of £300,000 in the 1991–92 season, effectively as third choice behind Peter Shilton and Martin Taylor. He had to bide his time and eventually got his chance, although was never able to fully establish himself but took over when Martin Taylor suffered a broken leg at Southend. He was appointed as club captain and began the promotion season of 1995–96 as first choice, but was substituted at half-time in a League game at Sheffield United in October 1995, which was to be his last game. Sutton was then sent on loan to Reading and given a free transfer to Birmingham City at the start of the 1996–97 season.

COSENZA 0
DERBY COUNTY 3

Anglo-Italian Cup, International Stage   **Tuesday 24 November 1992**

San Vito Stadium, Cosenza

Cosenza: Graziani, Balleri, Marino, Napoli (Lasacco, 56), Bia, Gazzaneo, Monza (Signorelli, 36), De Rosa, Negri, Fabris, Statuto. Other subs: Maritato, Napolitano, Fiore.
Derby County: Sutton, Comyn, Forsyth, Coleman, Wassall (Kavanagh, 45), Pembridge, Johnson, Williams, Kitson, Gabbiadini, McMinn. Other subs: Micklewhite, M. Taylor, Goulooze, Nicholson.
Referee: A. Buksh (London)
Attendance: 4,263

There was an Inter-League game in 1991 between the English and Italian second tiers that led to the resurrection of the Anglo-Italian Cup. The tournament was originally played in the early 1970s before a lack of interest caused it to be dropped to non-League status before it disappeared altogether.

After beating Notts County (home) and Barnsley (away) in the preliminary round, The Rams qualified for the European stages of the competition, their first competitive European match since the UEFA Cup tie against AEK Athens in the 1976–77 season. Their first trip was to Cosenza, based in the southern Italian region of Calabria, and the fans and players were greeted with pleasant, warm sunshine even though it was late November.

Cosenza had missed promotion to Serie A by just one point the previous season and had won their latest game at the weekend 2–0 at Verona and were lying fifth in the League. The San Vito Stadium was a typical continental stadium with a small main stand and the players entrance behind goal, down a flight of steps and a tunnel into the dressing rooms. One end of the stadium was under re-construction when Derby visited, who were chasing their seventh successive away victory.

Derby had been beaten at home by Sunderland at the weekend and were forced into several team changes for the Cup tie. Craig Short and Martin Kuhl were Cup tied as they had already played for other clubs before joining Derby. Simon Coleman and Paul Williams came into the starting line up and Paul Simpson had picked up an ankle injury that kept him out of the team.

Anglo Italian Cup 1992-93

Cosenza v Derby County

San Vito Stadium
Tuesday 24th November 1992
Kick-off 8.30 p.m.

Roy McFarland said 'obviously it is nice to be back in Europe; its nice to be playing against a different style of football. It gives us a little bit of a deeper insight into our players and how they react in this kind of environment.'

Cosenza included a young Marco Negri in their team. Walter Smith paid £3.5 million for him in his transfer from Perugia to Rangers in 1997, having scored 19 goals in 34 games for Cosenza. In 2004 he had a trial with Derby but was not offered a contract. The club was still in shock following the death of their midfield player Catena in a car crash in September.

Cosenza played in Crystal Palace-type colours of red-and-blue stripes, while Derby played in their normal white shirts and black shorts. The game had barely started when the first booking of the night came. Surprisingly, it was Paul Williams who made a two-footed challenge on a Cosenza player on the edge of his own penalty area and was rightly booked by the English referee Busch.

Derby took the lead on eight minutes. Ted McMinn was always likely to cause problems down the left wing with his awkward running style, and the first chance he had to run he was body-checked by the full-back. The free-kick was hit long, and the goalkeeper knocked the ball out for a corner and then did the same from a Johnson cross. The second corner was cleared out to Pembridge on the right wing, and his first-time high, forward ball caught the Cosenza defenders rushing out as Derby had Williams, Kitson, Coleman and Comyn following the ball. Andy Comyn was the furthest forward, and with no suspicion of offside he beat the goalkeeper on the penalty spot and the ball bounced into an empty net.

Cosenza defender Balleri picked up an early booking, inevitably on McMinn as the winger pushed the ball past him and was upended as he chased after the ball. McMinn needed lengthy treatment, and Roy McFarland came onto the field to check on the player, no doubt with instructions to keep going at the full-back as he will have to be very careful for the remaining 80 minutes.

The home team had not really caused Derby's defence too many issues as yet, and on 18 minutes Derby extended their lead. An excellent crossfield ball from Gabbiadini released Tommy Johnson on the right, but the goalkeeper came out of the area and sliced his attempted clearance out for a throw in. A Pembridge long throw was headed straight back out to him. He immediately sent the ball back into the danger area, and Kitson beat the goalkeeper to the ball some eight yards from goal and steered it into the net.

Just three minutes later the game was wrapped up following another poor clearance from the home defence. Paul Williams got the ball in space and, after a quick look up, chipped the ball over the defence and left Gabbiadini with a clear run on goal. A hard, low, shot to the centre of the goal gave the 200 noisy Derby fans something else to cheer as they now had a 3–0 lead.

An ugly, very high tackle from Statuto on Wassall brought another booking for the Italians. The injury kept Wassall from coming out for the second half, and he was replaced by Kavanagh. He was then on crutches on the journey back home through airports in Lamezia Terme, Italy and the East Midlands and missed the following three matches.

Having scored three goals in the first half, Derby did not have to do anything spectacular in the second half, just keep their heads, as Cosenza would not be happy at the way the game was going. There was some controversy on 55 minutes as Johnson was sent sprawling on turf in front of the dug outs by one of the players booked in the first half. The Italian players surrounded the referee, knowing that he had already been booked and was surely to be sent off. After a delay, the referee produced a second yellow card for the same player. The look of relief on his face was clear to see.

The Derby bench were livid, and the player was substituted very quickly before the referee realised his mistake. Derby players were being very professional, being under instructions to keep out of trouble as they were being provoked by the Italian tactics. There were a number of young players in the Derby side some of whom would not have experienced anything like this intimidation before.

The second half was full of niggly fouls and fortunately Derby's defence had little to do, the Cosenza team lacking any real goalscoring threat and were not able to produce a telling pass whenever they got within shooting distance. This meant they were restricted to long-range shots, which failed to trouble Steve Sutton.

Arthur Cox commented that 'everything about our trip was very enjoyable and the hospitality extended to us throughout was first class, except, of course between 8.30pm and 10.15pm on Tuesday evening'.

And of the travelling fans he said 'their help was appreciated and their company throughout the trip was nice to have.'

Michael Forsyth, Derby's captain, said the second half was 'one of the most unpleasant 45 minutes I have ever endured. The second half was horrible...provocation, body checking, spitting.'

There have not been many occasions when an English team has gone to Italy and won 3–0. Derby were to repeat the feat again three weeks later when they won at Reggiana by the same scoreline, in a game that was nearly postponed due to the foggy conditions prevailing in and around the Po Valley during mid-December.

In June 2004 financial troubles meant that Cosenza were in breach of Italian League regulations and were excluded from the League. A new club was formed in 2005 and has started playing in the lower, regional leagues.

TED MCMINN

Born: 28 September 1962

Debut v Portsmouth (away), Division One, 6 February 1988, lost 1–2

Last game v Wolverhampton Wanderers (home), Division One, 8 May 1993, won 2–0
First goal v Manchester United (home), Division One, 10 February 1988, lost 1–2
Bought from: Seville, Spain
Sold to: Birmingham City
Total appearances: 137 + 16 subs, 14 goals
Consecutive games: 30 from 10 September 1988 to 11 February 1989

The first transfer involving Ted McMinn from Glenafton to Queen of the South resulted in a fee of a new carpet for the club house and 1,000 lottery tickets. After a successful time at Rangers he followed his manager, Jock Wallace (son of a former Derby goalkeeper), out to Spain to play for Seville.

He was signed by Arthur Cox (who had been an admirer of him for several years) on 5 February 1988 for £300,000 and made his debut the following day at Portsmouth and scored a stunning goal on his home debut against Manchester United the following week. He quickly became a firm favourite with the fans with his unorthodox running style and ability.

Ted was on the verge of breaking into the Scotland squad when a bad tackle in a game at Tottenham Hotspur in November 1989 put him on the sidelines for over a year.

1991–92 saw him back to his best and voted Player of the Year in a season that saw The Rams reach the Play-off semi-finals.

In July 1993 he was transferred to Birmingham City. After brief spells as assistant manager to Mark Wright, he returned to Derby and became the match summariser for Radio Derby. Having had the lower part of his right leg amputated after an infection caught while on holiday, a benefit game was staged for him on 1 May 2006 between Derby and Rangers legends that drew a record Pride Park crowd of 33,475 (including over 12,000 from Scotland).

BRENTFORD 3
DERBY COUNTY 4

Anglo-Italian Cup, semi-final, first leg   **Wednesday 27 January 1993**

Griffin Park

Brentford: Benstead, Bennett, Mortimer, Millen, Statham, Manuel, Allon, Chalmers (Buckle, 84), Godfrey, Blissett, Luscombe (Gayle, 84). Other subs: Bates, Jones, Bayes.
Derby County: Sutton, Kavanagh, Forsyth, Coleman, Wassall, Pembridge, Johnson, Comyn, Kitson, Gabbiadini, Patterson. Subs: Micklewhite, M. Taylor, Simpson, Hayward, Nicholson.
Referee: A. Gunn (South Chailey)
Attendance: 5,227

After both teams topped their respective groups (Derby beating West Ham United and Bristol City after their games against Cremonese, Cosenza and Reggiana; Brentford overcoming Portsmouth, Birmingham City and Newcastle United and the Italian teams Ascoli, Lucchese and Cesena), the teams met in a two-legged semi-final, the first leg being at Griffin Park. Brentford's record in the competition was the best of all the teams, with a 100 per cent winning sequence from their six matches. Derby had not won at Griffin Park since 5 October 1946 when they won 3–0.

Derby were still suffering from the fact the Craig Short and Martin Kuhl were Cup

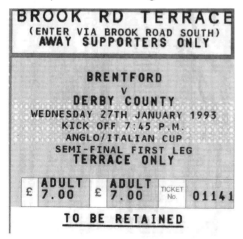

tied in the competition and injuries also ruled out Paul Williams, Ted McMinn and Richard Goulooze from the midfield area. That meant a rare start for Mark Patterson, who last made an appearance at Barnsley in September and would have joined Preston North End if they had not sacked their manager halfway through the discussions. Simon Coleman came in for Cup tied Craig Short once again in the centre of defence.

Derby had just played an FA Cup tie the previous Saturday, away at Luton Town, which they had won 5–1, while Brentford were in League action with a 0–1 defeat at Portsmouth, this being their fourth successive defeat. Actually, their last win of any kind was the Boxing Day 2–1 victory over Derby. In terms of League positions, there was just one point separating them, with Derby having the advantage.

Derby decided to play with three centre halves of Coleman, Wassall and Comyn to counteract the physical forwards of Brentford. Derby's forward line of Gabbiadini, Johnson and Kitson was a match for any defence and the pace and movement they had between them would likely cause the Brentford defence some difficulty.

Derby's away performances in the last round of the Anglo-Italian Cup had been impressive, winning both by a scoreline of 3–0, scoring all their goals early in the game. The travelling band of 750 Derby fans came hoping to see a repeat of the other away fixtures in this competition.

The semi-final followed the same pattern when Mark Patterson shot into the corner of the net from the edge of the area on eight minutes. The opportunity was made when Paul Kitson's right-wing cross was laid back by Tommy Johnson.

Just two minutes later, Derby extended the lead. A long kick by Steve Sutton was allowed to reach Johnson, who found Kitson, again in a wide position. His cross went over Bennett and came to Gabbiadini who had time to chest the ball down, take a couple of steps and fire the ball past 'keeper Benstead.

Brentford's only threat at this time was from free-kicks or corners, where they could target the physical presence of Joe Allon and Gary Blissett. Allon was Brentford's record signing, £275,000 from Chelsea in November.

The Rams were 3–0 up in the 27th minute when a long throw by Mark Pembridge forced Mortimer in the Brentford defence into an error and left Paul Kitson with an opportunity that he converted with some ease. That was his 17th goal of the season.

Once again, Derby found themselves 3–0 up after 30 minutes and should have had the game well under control. This being the semi-final, though, Brentford were not going to give in as easily as the Italian opponents from previous rounds.

On 38 minutes, following a succession of corners, the latest one was taken by Manuel was headed on by Gary Blissett and Joe Allon was the player to jump the highest at the far post and give Brentford something to cheer about before the break.

Just on the stroke of half-time, Allon notched his second goal and set up the second half. Darren Wassall fouled Blissett, who took the free-kick himself. The free-kick was low and hard, which Sutton could only parry into the path of Allon, who scored with glee.

Tommy Johnson, could and should have put the game and tie beyond any doubt as three times he had been put through by Pembridge. The first chance was deflected wide, Benstead came out well to block him for the second and the last hit Benstead's legs. Chances were also being created at an alarming rate at the Derby end, despite their three centre-halves, with Allon and Luscombe both forcing saves from Sutton.

Derby gained some breathing space on 75 minutes when a Pembridge corner was not cleared by the home team and Patterson following up had one shot blocked and followed up himself to smack the ball under the goalkeeper to give Derby a 4–2 lead.

As much as Patterson was the hero at one end of the field with his unexpected two goals, Steve Sutton was equally heroic in the Derby goal by pulling off several fine saves as Brentford continued pressing for another goal. He was eventually beaten with just five minutes remaining when Allon completed his hat-trick, heading in a Manuel free-kick to set up a grandstand finish, capitalising on some slack defending.

Johnson had yet another opportunity late on when put through by Gabbiadini, but the shot this time was straight at the 'keeper. The Derby manager said the game was 'a truly entertaining and exciting encounter'.

The Brentford manager revealed afterwards that 'Joe Allon was rubbish in training yesterday – I just hope he will have a few more bad sessions'.

As Gerald Mortimer commented 'There were enough incidents and ingredients in the game to fill a book. Some of the defending was enough to turn managers grey overnight, but there was deadly finishing from two teams flat out for the Final. The outcome was magnificent entertainment: no eye could stray for fear of missing another definitive moment.'

Derby's single-goal lead set up the second leg a fortnight later and, with Brentford having nothing to lose, a fascinating game was in store. Brentford were bouyed by the fact they had scored three times against Derby and won the second leg at the Baseball Ground 2–1. Gabbiadini had given Derby the lead just before half-time, and all seemed well until the last eight minutes when two goals from Gary Blissett turned the game around and had people reaching for the rule book. This made the scores 5–5 on aggregate, and with no extra-time scheduled in the tie Derby won through to their first Wembley appearance since 1975, courtesy of the away goals rule.

The day after the game, Tim Ward, former Rams player died in a Burton hospital. He rejoined as Derby manager in 1962 and was responsible for signing Kevin Hector, Alan Durban, Colin Boulton, Ron Webster (all of whom were selected in Derby's all-time team, confirmed during 2009) among many others.

MARK PATTERSON

Born: 13 September 1968
First game v Bournemouth (home), Simod Cup, 9 November 1988, won 1–0
Last game v Wolverhampton Wanderers (home), Division Two, 8 May 1993, won 2–0

First goal v Norwich City (away), Division One, 22 September 1990, lost 1–2

Bought from: Carlisle United

Sold to: Plymouth Argyle

Total appearances: 55 + 13 subs, 5 goals

Consecutive games: 10 from 10 February 1993 to 17 March 1993

Patterson began his professional career at Carlisle United and, after just 22 games for them, he was signed by Derby for £85,000 as a squad player. He had to wait for a year before making his first-team debut. He was injured for several months, during which time other players had come in and staked their claim for his place either as right-back or midfield.

Probably the goal of his career was a superb shot in an FA Cup replay against Burnley that was struck from the record books as the game was abandoned due to fog.

In July 1993 he was sold to Plymouth for £60,000 and played there for four years before moving to Gillingham for a further five years.

DERBY COUNTY 3
SHEFFIELD WEDNESDAY 3

FA Cup sixth round   **Monday 8 March 1993**

Baseball Ground

Derby County: Taylor, Patterson, Forsyth, Nicholson, Short, Pembridge, Williams, Kuhl, Kitson, Gabbiadini, Johnson. Subs: Goulooze, Comyn.
Sheffield Wednesday: Woods, Nisson, Worthington, Palmer, Harkes (Jemson, 80), Anderson, Wilson, Waddle, Warhurst, Bright, Sheridan (Hyde, 57).
Referee: G.R. Ashby (Worcester)
Attendance: 22,511

Derby had beaten Stockport County (2–1 at home), Luton Town (5–1 away) and Bolton Wanderers (3–1 at home) to reach the sixth round of the FA Cup, one win away from a semi-final appearance being staged for the first time at Wembley Stadium. The Owls had won 2–1 at Cambridge United, 1–0 at home to Sunderland and 2–0 at home to Southend United.

It was a case of déja vu as The Rams and Sheffield Wednesday were paired together for the fifth time in seven years in the two major domestic Cup competitions. The omens on that basis were not good, as only once had Derby come out on top, that in the 1989–90 League Cup competition.

Derby were lying in ninth place in Division One, mainly thanks to their away record. Their home form was really that of a relegation team, having lost 10 of the 16 League games played so far, making it a club record for losing the most home games since joining the League in 1888.

Wednesday, however, were in fourth place in the Premier League and were already in the semi-finals of

the League Cup and had just won the first leg 4–2 away at Blackburn Rovers. Derby fans turned up in force once again, despite the fact that this was the eighth home game out of the last nine games played.

Craig Short had scored in all of the previous rounds, a record he would be looking to continue and strive for a Cup Final place (or at least a semi-final place to get him to

Wembley), especially as he would be Cup tied for the Anglo-Italian Cup Final later in the month. As well as Short, there was only Ian Wright of Arsenal who could still score in every round of the competition, a feat which had not been achieved since Peter Osgood in the 1969–70 season.

Any match under the lights at the Baseball Ground always seem to heighten the atmosphere, and when there is a large, vocal crowd as well, then it gives the younger fans a glimpse of what the atmosphere used to be like during the early 1970s, when crowds regularly topped 40,000. The game was staged on a Monday night for the benefit of a live TV broadcast by SKY, instead of the scheduled date of the Saturday – one of Derby's first home games to be shown by that broadcaster.

Derby welcomed Mark Pembridge and Martin Kuhl back into the starting line up, replacing Richard Goulooze and Steve Hayward who had filled in while they were absent. Martin Kuhl, although far from being match fit, had his left thigh heavily strapped and was an important, experienced figure in the centre of the midfield, and it was decided to risk him.

For Sheffield Wednesday, Danny Wilson was a surprise name on the team sheet just two weeks after breaking two ribs. Chris Waddle had been signed during the previous close season for £1 million from Marseille, and he was the main influence on the game in the opening stages of the game and, despite being closely marked by a couple of players, he was still able to show that extra quality that seemed to give him that extra bit of time and space to dictate the pace and course of the game.

In the first half, Wednesday were attacking the Osmaston End, where their enthusiastic fans were congregated, welcoming the teams onto the field with a shower of yellow and blue balloons. The first goal of the game came from a penalty to the Owls after 12 minutes. Mark Patterson clipped Mark Bright's heels as he chased a Waddle pass and, although he was trying to avoid contact, any sort of contact in the penalty area is likely to be punished with a penalty. John Sheridan put the penalty right in the corner, even though Martin Taylor got his fingertips to the ball.

Derby drew level with a superb shot from Nicholson. It all started with a clearance from Martin Taylor aimed towards Gabbiadini in the centre circle. He was fouled by Viv Anderson, who then stopped Derby taking the free-kick quickly, for which he was shown a yellow card. Gabbiadini was also cautioned as he pushed Anderson in an attempt to wrestle the ball from the defender. Kuhl took the free-kick inside the centre circle and knocked the ball to Nicholson, and looking up there were no Sheffield Wednesday players between him and the penalty area, everyone expecting the free-kick to be launched forwards.

After running a few yards and still more than 35 yards out, he unleashed an unstoppable shot that flew past everyone, including Chris Woods in the Wednesday goal. The ball smacked against the cross bar and caught the 'keeper on his legs as it bounced down and back into the net. Technically an own goal, no one wanted to take it away from Nicholson in only his fourth appearance.

Derby were level for just seven minutes as Waddle again played a part in the goal – this time playing a ball through the Derby defence to Paul Warhurst, the central defender, turned striker, who placed the ball past Taylor like a seasoned forward.

At 2–1 down at the interval, Derby took the half-time break to adjust and started the second half on the front foot with several dangerous shots coming in towards the Wednesday goal from Johnson, Patterson and Gabbiadini. The first half would have given the players some encouragement that Wednesday were not unbeatable and with a bit more belief and conviction a result could be achieved.

Wednesday were forced into a change on 57 minutes when Nicholson went in heavily on Sheridan who could not continue and was replaced by Hyde and before he could get into the pace of the game, Derby got a second equaliser a couple of minutes later. From a Chris Woods goalkick, the ball was initially won by Paul Williams whose forward header was helped on by Paul Kitson, who found Gabbiadini. His control and turn left the lumbering Palmer trailing behind him. As he ran into the penalty area, Palmer and Anderson were both closing him down but he let fly a right foot shot that flew past Woods into the roof of the net

Derby took the lead for the first time in the tie on 74 minutes. Nicholson, put in by Pembridge crossed and it landed on the head of Kitson who buried the ball.

As the last 10 minutes approached, Wednesday made their final change with Nigel Jemson, formerly of rivals Nottingham Forest, in place of John Harkes and within four minutes he had made an impact.

Jemson broke on another glorious pass from Waddle and pulled back a cross for Warhurst to score decisively. That was his 11th goal in 10 games – not a bad return for a converted defender.

With time running out and the prospect of a replay at Hillsborough, both teams were trying to win. Wednesday would want to avoid a fixture pile-up, being well placed in the League and on course for a League Cup Final place. Waddle was aggrieved when Nicholson seemed to tug him back, and a fierce low cross from Waddle squirmed away from Taylor as Bright challenged.

The *Derby Evening Telegraph* report said 'Derby County and Sheffield Wednesday studded last night's throbbing FA Cup sixth round tie at the Baseball Ground with brilliant goals.

'The match became better as the night wore on. Derby, tame in the first half, pounded forward after the interval and their players grew in stature. Marco Gabbiadini, for example. He was so strong and competitive, he covered a phenomenal amount of ground and he scored a great goal. Paul Williams was colossal and Shane Nicholson, only four games into a senior career at Derby, has taken his chance wonderfully well'.

The view from Sheffield was similar, their programme for the replay saying 'there was no shortage of goals or excitement at a fiercely partisan Baseball Ground with the result uncertain to the final whistle', and captain Nigel Pearson said 'they came out playing with a lot more self belief in the second half. We stuck to our task very well, and could still have won it at the end.'

The old statistic that Derby had not won at Hillsborough since September 1936 was banded around the media, as if it was a forgone conclusion that Derby would be beaten. In the event, Wednesday won the replay 1–0 with another goal from Warhurst.

Wednesday had reached the Final of the League Cup on the Sunday before the replay, and went to Wembley before losing to Arsenal. They also went on to the FA Cup Final at Wembley, after beating neighbours Sheffield United in the semi-final, and drew with Arsenal and took part in the last FA Cup Final replay game a few days later, which they lost 2–1 after extra time. It is not often a club side will visit Wembley four times in less than 50 days, as the Owls did. The disappointing thing for them was that they only won one of those games.

SHANE NICHOLSON

Born: 3 June 1970
Debut v Leicester City (home), Division Two, 24 February 1993, won 2–0
Last game v Port Vale (away), Division Two, 20 January 1996, draw 1–1
First goal v Sheffield Wednesday, (FA Cup), 8 March 1993, draw 3–3
Bought from: Lincoln City
Sold to: West Bromwich Albion
Total appearances: 86 + 1 sub, 2 goals
Consecutive games: 21 from 22 January 1994 to 8 May 1994

Nicholson was signed from Lincoln City on 22 April 1992, for a fee of £100,000, where he had made over 130 appearances, during which time he had helped them back into the League following the demotion to the Vauxhall Conference.

He was not a regular in the starting line-up, although he played in the majority of games in the latter half of the 1992–93 season, including an appearance in the Anglo-Italian Cup Final at Wembley.

The arrival of Chris Powell made his first-team chances less likely and on 9 February 1996 he joined rivals West Bromwich Albion, for a fee of £150,000, where again he was not a regular and suffered injuries. He was banned for several months from football for drug abuse.

DERBY COUNTY 1 CREMONESE 3

Anglo-Italian Cup Final   **Saturday 27 March 1993**

Wembley Stadium

Derby County: Taylor, Patterson, Forsyth, Nicholson, Coleman, Pembridge, Micklewhite, Goulooze (Hayward, 83), Kitson, Gabbiadini, Johnson (Simpson, 81). Other subs: Sutton, Comyn, Stallard.
Cremonese: Turci, Gualco, Pedroni, Cristiani, Colonnese, Verdelli, Giandebiaggi, Nicolini, Tentoni (Montorfano, 85), Maspero, Florjancic (Dezotti, 73). Other subs: Violini, Feraroni, Lombardini.
Referee: Joaquim Urio Velasquez (Tolosa, Spain)
Attendance: 37,024

After the European rounds of the competition, Derby and Brentford were to play in the English Final and Cremonese and Bari played each other in Italy to decide which clubs would contest the Final. The 'international stage', as it was officially described by the League, had produced 80 goals and 18 sendings off and 79 bookings in the 32 matches.

The Final of this, the first, resurrected competition was to be played at Wembley Stadium with a 1.30pm kick-off, with the game being shown live on the RAI Uno Italian television channel, as their normal match day was a Sunday. There were no Premier League matches over the weekend, so this fixture was the biggest game in the country.

Cremonese had already beaten Derby 3–1 in the earlier round at the Baseball Ground, which was Derby's only defeat in this year's competition. Cremonese beat Bari 6–3 on aggregate, winning the home leg 4–1 and drawing the return game 2–2 to reach the Final.

The Wembley Stadium capacity had been reduced down to 80,000 following the all-seat recommendations of the Taylor Report that ultimately was the reason for the plethora of new stadium builds and the re-

ANGLO ITALIAN CUP
COPPA ANGLO
ITALIANA

CREMONESE

V

DERBY COUNTY

SATURDAY 27
MARCH 1993
KICK-OFF 1.30PM
OFFICIAL
MATCHDAY
PROGRAMME
£3.00

building of the national stadium, although its location in a crowded north suburb in London was still not ideal.

As the number of travelling Italian supporters was likely to be quite small, Derby's allocation was up to 60,000, with prices ranging from £11 to £26. No more than 1,000

Italians were expected to attend having made the 800-mile journey from northern Italy, although many London-based Italians would likely cheer on their team.

Derby's last appearance at Wembley was the 2–0 win against West Ham United in the Charity Shield in August 1975, and the stadium had changed little in 18 years – the outside was still shabby, the seats uncomfortable and the view spoilt by the ring of posts going around the stadium holding up the roof, and facilities overall not very good.

Cremonese, were top of Serie B, and destined for promotion to the top tier of football in Italy and were the bookmakers' pre-match favourites to take the trophy. They had a talented forward line of Slovenian Matjaz Florjancic (who was the leading scorer in the competition) and Andrea Tentoni (the then Serie B top scorer).

For many of Derby's players this was their first time at Wembley as a player and for some the biggest game of their careers and a new experience. Gary Micklewhite had played in an FA Cup Final for Queen's Park Rangers and Paul Simpson with Oxford United.

Derby still had the Cup-tied players, but there were several other injury worries as well – Mark Patterson had a rib injury with Steve Round standing by to replace him. Marco Gabbiadini was suffering with ankle and thigh injuries and under constant treatment from physiotherapist Gordon Guthrie.

Richard Goolooze was handed just his fourth start since his move from Heerenveen in September 1992 for £100,000, coming in for Kuhl to make use of his passing ability on the wide Wembley pitch. With Kuhl out, the captaincy reverted back to Michael Forsyth who joined previous captains Jack Nicholas and Roy McFarland in leading out the Rams at Wembley. All the Derby players that were doubtful, declared themselves fit to play – amazing what a Wembley Final will do for clearing up injuries!

Cremonese and Derby had met each other in the earlier rounds of the competition, with the Italians winning 3–1 at the Baseball Ground, Derby's only defeat so far in the competition. Attendances in Italy had been poor and with all the costs of air fares and hotels, Derby had to reach the Final to stand a chance of making any profit.

Cremonese kicked-off and immediately caused a number of problems with some dangerous probing runs from their dangerous front pair of Florjancic and Tentoni. After 11 minutes Cremonese took a deserved lead. Coleman stopped a run from Tentoni to concede a corner, and Patterson headed that out for another corner. Florjancic took the corner and this time curled the ball right under the bar, which was met by former Inter Milan defender Verdelli who bundled the ball past Taylor.

Derby had a couple of half chances as Johnson shot into the side netting and Coleman headed wide, but overall The Rams were struggling to cope with the Italians. The first booking came on 18 minutes as Johnson, targeted as a possible dangerman, was fouled by Maspero. There was no doubt about the booking, and the tackle left Johnson holding his knee in some discomfort.

Five minutes later, Derby equalised. Patterson picked the ball up and ran through the central midfield area before releasing Kitson on the left. His first-time cross was superbly headed by Gabbiadini, whose father is Italian, into the goal, via a post. Gary Micklewhite found a good position and was picked out by another Kitson cross. His shot was slightly mis-timed and he hit it into the ground and that took all the power out of the shot.

In what turned out to be an eventful first half, Cremonese were awarded a penalty on 28 minutes when Forsyth, the Derby captain, made a bad tackle from behind on Giandebiaggi. There were no arguments about the decision, and Nicolini hit his shot well into the corner. Martin Taylor joined a select few goalkeepers that had saved a penalty at Wembley Stadium to keep the scores level.

Chances continued to be created by the Italians, with Taylor stopping everything that was coming his way. At the other end there were only sporadic Derby attacks, but despite the crosses being put over and free-kicks given they were unable to get a clear shot on target.

The Italians had a superior passing technique and were pulling the Derby midfield and defence around in order to create an opportunity. The game had been a contrast of styles, as usual the continental players had better technique, vision and pace where Derby were relying on hard work, a rigid system and strength.

There was an early chance in the second half for Derby as Micklewhite's fine run found Gabbiadini, and he was brought down just outside the penalty area. Pembridge took the free-kick and he curled it just the wrong side of the post.

A second penalty was awarded by the Spanish referee to Cremonese on 50 minutes as Tentoni got past Forsyth and fell over Martin Taylor as he came out to block the ball. Unlike the first penalty, this one was a debatable decision with the Derby players complaining bitterly. Maspero took responsibility this time and made sure the ball was out of the reach of the goalkeeper. Martin Taylor to this day remains convinced that he did not touch the Italian forward.

The Cremonese defenders were using all their experience and off-the-ball tactics to unsettle the Derby players, and to a large extent it had worked in their favour. Gabbiadini was the most lively Derby forward, his bustling, physical style upsetting the stern Italian defence and there were some strong calls for a Derby penalty when Luigi Gualco seemed to foul him in the box. These two players finally had enough with each other and both were booked just before the hour mark following an off the ball incident. Not all the bad challenges were from Cremonese – Shane Nicholson was lucky to escape with just a booking when he went in with a thigh-high challenge on Matjaz Florjancic.

With 20 minutes to go the game should have been all over as Florjancic broke the off-side trap, and although he had Giandebaggi up in support and unmarked in the centre of the goal he decided to shoot himself and put the ball into the side netting.

Gustavo Dezotti was brought on to replace Flojancic – Dezotti was the top scorer the previous season and gained 'fame' in the 1990 World Cup Final when he became the second of the Argentinians to be sent off in the game against Germany. As one reporter said at the time, bringing him on 'was akin to hosing down a blaze with gasoline'.

Some of the Italian's antics and professional and personal attacks were getting too much, with Kitson being stamped on in full view of the referee. Mark Pembridge did not fare any better, being punched while offering to help up Dezotti, following a Micklewhite foul soon after he had come on. The punch left Pembridge with a mark underneath his left eye for a number of days afterwards, but again Dezotti was not booked.

Another opportunity to put the game beyond Derby came and went on 78 minutes when Tentoni pulled the ball back for Nicolini. He beat Taylor with his shot, but the ball hit the post and bounced away to safety. Eventually, after 83 minutes and with Derby tiring, Cremonese got the third goal they deserved when the impressive Tentoni chased a through ball, beat Forsyth for pace and shot under Taylor from an angle.

Despite some of the questionable refereeing decisions and predictable off-the-ball incidents, the general consensus was that the Italians were the better team on the day and deserved the win, especially as they had already beaten The Rams at the Baseball Ground earlier in the competition.

Arthur Cox admitted that 'their quality was too much for what we had and Cremonese certainly deserved to win. We did not do ourselves justice'.

With over 36,000 Derby fans inside Wembley, chairman Brian Fearn said 'our fans were magnificent but we were beaten by a better team.'

Cremonese's main objective of the 1992–93 season was to secure promotion to Serie A, which was achieved, and the following season they finished a respectable 10th position. Some of the players went on to play for bigger and better teams.

The attendance of 37,024 was only beaten anywhere in the UK by that of Rangers in the Scottish League.

MICHAEL FORSYTH

Born: 20 March 1966
Debut v Oldham Athletic (home), Division Two, 23 August 1986, lost 0–1
Last game v Sheffield United (home), Division Two, 4 February 1995, lost 2–3

First goal v Sunderland (home), Division Two, 1 October 1986, won 3–2

Bought from: West Bromwich Albion

Sold to: Notts County

Total appearances: 403 + 3 subs, 10 goals

Consecutive games: 125 from 30 April 1988 to 5 January 1991

Forsyth started his career at West Bromwich Albion but failed to gain a regular place in their starting line-up. He was bought on transfer deadline day of 1986 for £25,000 and was seen as the long-term replacement for the long-serving Steve Buckley. He made his first-team debut on opening day fixture of the 1986–87 season (along with Mel Sage, Mark Lillis and Steve Cross) and ended in defeat, the only home defeat of the Division Two Championship season.

His consistent and reliable performances against the leading players in the country gained him England Under-21 and B honours, and he was also voted Player of the Year in the 1987–88 season. He was captain of the two Wembley teams in the Anglo-Italian Cup Final in 1993 and Division One Play-off Final in 1994 and was sold just six months before a testimonial would have been due.

He moved to Notts County on 23 February 1995 for £200,000 and later was signed by his former teammate John Gregory at Wycombe Wanderers.

DERBY COUNTY 1 LEICESTER CITY 2

Play-off Final   **Monday 30 May 1994**

Wembley Stadium

Derby County: Taylor, Charles, Forsyth (Kitson, 87), Harkes, Short, Williams, Cowans, Johnson, Gabbiadini, Pembridge, Simpson. Other subs: Sutton, Kavanagh.
Leicester City: Ward, Grayson, Whitlow, Willis, Coatsworth (Thompson, 68), Carey, Gibson, Blake, Walsh, Roberts (Joachim, 56), Ormondroyd. Other sub: Poole.
Referee: R.G. Milford (Bristol)
Attendance: 73,671

After 46 League games and two Play-off semi-final matches, the whole season came down to one match, with the possibility of extra time and penalties.

It was a good season for the East Midlands teams, with Nottingham Forest finishing second behind Crystal Palace and Derby and Leicester finishing in the top six places. Leicester had finished fourth, with Derby in the last Play-off place just two points behind. Derby had beaten Millwall in an eventful semi-final second leg.

There were lots of connections between the two clubs – Leicester's assistant manager was John Gregory (former Derby player during the mid-to-late 1980s), and Leicester also had Ian Ormondroyd and Phil Gee available for selection, both players exchanged for Paul Kitson. Leicester were back on familiar territory having lost their two previous Play-off Finals to Blackburn Rovers and to Swindon Town the previous year.

Leicester's season had been disrupted by injuries throughout the campaign, with 12 players being ruled out at one stage, including key players like Steve Walsh, who had been out since September, and Roberts who had missed recent games due to cracked ribs.

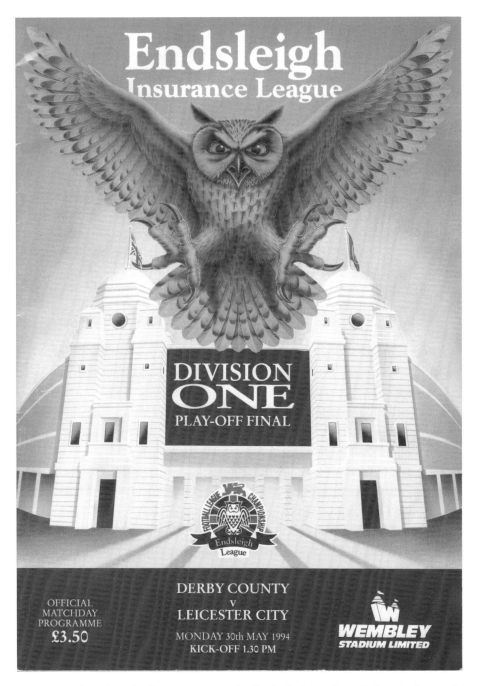

Current form from both teams was good – Derby had just three defeats in the last 17 games, while Leicester were unbeaten in the last 11 games, although eight of those were draws. Derby's John Harkes was due to fly out immediately after the game to join the USA World Cup squad for the tournament that was to be played in his home country.

There were high hopes for a good game, with 11 goals being scored in the two games (3–3 at Filbert Street and a 3–2 win for Derby at the Baseball Ground) between the clubs in the regular League season. There were two contrasting styles – Leicester hoping to out-muscle and out-jump the Derby defence with the tall presence of Walsh, Roberts and Ormondroyd against the pace of the Derby forwards of Johnson and Gabbiadini. Steve Walsh had been missing for most of the season through injury, playing just one game in the last seven months.

One of the most respected referees was to take charge of the game. Roger Milford, who had reached the age limit for referees, was forced to retire, and so this was to be his last game.

This Play-off fixture was even more important than any other that had gone before as the following season only one team from the second tier would be promoted, along with the Play-off winners, while four teams were to be relegated to reduce the number of teams in the Premier League.

It was a very hot and sunny afternoon for the Bank Holiday game with the M1 full of supporters travelling down from the East Midlands.

Leicester picked Roberts over Joachim in the forward line, this to go up against Derby's midfielder turned centre-half Paul Williams, where they could see a potential weakness.

Just two minutes into the game, Derby came close to taking the lead – a long throw from Pembridge came to Tommy Johnson whose shot was blocked and not properly cleared and reached Gabbiadini. His shot was on target and beat the goalkeeper but not Willis who cleared off the line.

The early stages were being played at a very fast pace which, given the weather conditions, could not be kept up and the older players on each team, Cowans and Gibson in particular, would be expected to slow the game down.

On the quarter hour, Derby's plan to release Johnson at pace showed promising signs of success as a long, high ball over the defence from Simpson saw him free, with Ward in the Leicester goal coming out well to stop him. Not long afterwards, Derby should have taken the lead following a good move that started with Gary Charles on the edge of the Derby penalty area. He passed to Harkes who passed square to Pembridge who then launched the ball over the top again. This time it was Gabbiadini who broke and took the defenders with him, leaving Johnson all alone in the centre. Gabbiadini squeezed a pass along the penalty area line as he was closed down by the defence and Johnson hit his first-time shot wide of the 'keeper's left-hand post, when he could have had time to control it, stop and place the ball.

This was often a criticism of Johnson: if he had time to think about how and where to shoot, it was likely he would miss, whereas a chance out of the blue he

Paul Simpson evades a challenge from the Leicester defence.

would be more likely to score from.

Just four minutes after that close shave, a similar move worked to perfection. Another long ball from Simpson on the left on half-way left Johnson running between the two big central defenders. He out paced both of them, took one touch with his left foot and shot straight away with his right and into the net to give Derby a well-deserved lead.

Martin Taylor, the only Derby player to feature in all of the League games, was called into serious action six minutes before the break when Whitlow hit a shot from the edge of the area that came through a crowd of players and took a slight deflection. His flying save was only a temporary escape.

A high ball into the Derby area saw a clutch of players go for the ball – Short, Walsh, Roberts and Taylor. It looked like Roberts clearly impeded Taylor and Walsh got his head to the ball, but got no real power behind it. Williams on the goalline tried to head the ball away but was beaten by the bounce and spin of the ball and looked bemused as the ball ended in the net. It looked easier to clear the ball than not. It was Walsh's first goal for eight months and a predictable way of Leicester getting level – aiming high balls up for the big forwards to battle against the defenders.

Derby had an early chance at the start of the second half, made by Gabbiadini and Harkes who pulled the ball back for Johnson who beat the defenders but could not keep the ball down sufficiently. Another chance gone.

The most controversial moment in the game occurred on 61 minutes and a potential turning point. As in the first half, Simpson released Johnson down the left, completely free and heading for goal. Grayson came over, and as Johnson pushed the ball past him he was brought down. Derby fans were clearly calling for a red card for the defender as he was the last man. Unfortunately, the referee determined that Johnson did not have full control of the ball and was not denied a goalscoring opportunity.

Derby were generally in control of the game, but it had evened out in the second half. It was still the final ball that was letting them down when they got into good positions, and the crosses from wide were not quite good enough on the day.

Five minutes from time, two pieces of action settled the game. Firsty, Gordon Cowans played the ball into the Leicester box, and as Gibson and Harkes went for the ball Gibson slipped, leaving Harkes on his own. Unfortunately, the ball was running across the face of the area, and as he tried to screw his foot around the ball on his weaker left foot, it drifted wide of the goal.

A minute later, Leicester took the lead for the first time as Whitlow fired over a cross from the right wing and former Derby forward, Ian Ormondroyd, beat Short and Forsyth to the ball. His glancing header was brilliantly saved one handed by Taylor but left Gary Charles flat footed at the far post, and Walsh was on hand a couple of yards out to stab it over the line. Paul Kitson was immediately introduced, replacing Forsyth, but the goal came too late in the game to make any difference.

Chairman Lionel Pickering was very philosophical after the game. While obviously disappointed at the result, he was not totally unsurprised as the one thing Derby had been throughout the season was consistently inconsistent. There was going to have to be some trimming of the playing staff, and he expected to lose several members who wanted to try their hand in the Premier League.

The following season was always going to be difficult, as most losing finalists find, and it was six games into the season before The Rams won a game. The inconsistent form continued throughout the year, and a decision was made that Roy McFarland's contract would not be renewed at the end of the season, bringing an end to a long association with the club. At the same time many of the current playing staff's contracts were coming to an end and chose to leave.

TOMMY JOHNSON

Born: 15 January 1971
Debut v Tranmere Rovers (away), Division Two, 14 March 1992, lost 3–4
Last game v Sunderland (away), Division Two, 31 December 1994, draw 1–1
First goal v Plymouth Argyle (home), 24 March 1992, won 2–0

Bought from: Notts County
Sold to: Aston Villa
Total appearances: 121 + 8 subs, 41 goals
Consecutive appearances: 41 from 14 March 1992 to 6 December 1992

Tommy Johnson had been a prolific scorer for Notts County on their rise to the top division, having won two successive Play-offs, with a goal on average every 2.5 games. Derby now had money to spend and paid £1,375 million for him in March 1992. A year later Johnson was helping them to an Anglo-Italian Cup Final and then a Play-off Final, where he scored the opening goal (he had scored in two different Play-off Finals for Notts County) in a game Derby eventually lost.

The flame-haired forward was quick, always played with a smile and was one of those strikers that if there was time about where to shoot, he would probably miss, but shooting on instinct he was superb.

After the breakup of the Play-off team, Johnson was sold to Aston Villa for £1.45 million and went on to play for Celtic, Everton, Sheffield Wednesday, Kilmarnock, Gillingham, Sheffield United and Scunthorpe United. He scored a memorable goal for Gillingham on his first appearance at Pride Park in January 2004, a game Derby won 2–1.

BIRMINGHAM CITY 1
DERBY COUNTY 4

Division One   **Tuesday 21 November 1995**

St Andrews

Birmingham City: Bennett, Hiley, Cooper, Ward, Edwards, Johnson, Finnan (Hunt, 45), Claridge, Rushfeldt (Charlery, 45), Otto, Tait (Martin, 47).
Derby County: Hoult, Carsley, Boden, Powell (Flynn, 85), Yates, Stimac, van der Laan (Simpson, 87), Sturridge, Willems, Gabbiadini, Carsley. Other sub: S. Sutton.
Referee: K.J. Breen (Liverpool)
Attendance: 19,417

Derby's last away game, and also the debut of Croatian Igor Stimac, ended in a 5–1 defeat at Tranmere Rovers and left Derby in 17th place in the table, still trying to find some consistency and settled team selection in Jim Smith's rebuilding first season in charge. Two home victories over West Bromwich Albion (3–0) and Charlton Athletic (2–0) since that defeat saw them climb to eighth.

Birmingham City were on a very good run of form – 15 games unbeaten in all competitions, winning six out of the last eight League games, lying third in the table, and were strong favourites to take all three points from this mid-week fixture.

The Blues made two changes from the team that drew 0–0 at Luton Town on Saturday – Finnan replaced Jonathan Hunt and Rushfeldt replaced Ken Charlery. Jim Smith was able to name an unchanged line-up for the third successive game, the previous two matches bringing comfortable victories with no goals conceded. It was a clear and very cold night in Birmingham and the Rams fans had travelled down the A38 in large numbers.

Even in the early stages, Dean Sturridge had already threatened to run past defender Andy Edwards a couple of times and showed he could beat him for pace easily and it did not take long for Derby to show an extra piece of skill that brought the first goal after just four minutes.

Robin van der Laan and fellow Dutchman, Ron Willems won the ball in the middle of the Birmingham City half and played the ball forward to Gabbiadini who laid the ball back to van der Laan moving forward. Sturridge had lost his marker by a couple of

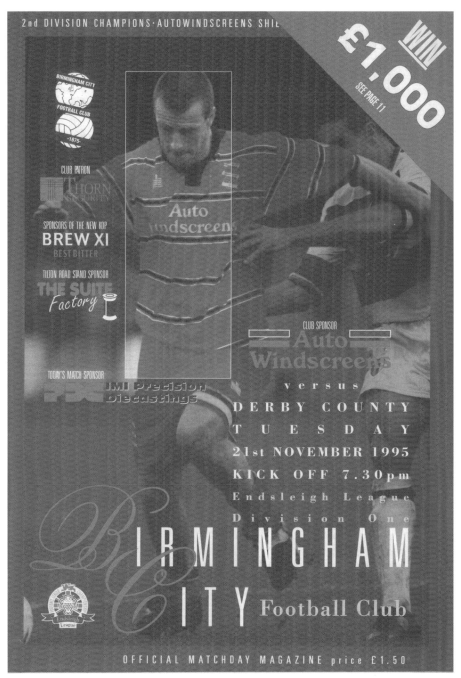

2nd DIVISION CHAMPIONS·AUTOWINDSCREENS SHIE

WIN £1,000 SEE PAGE 11

BIRMINGHAM CITY FOOTBALL CLUB -1875-

CLUB PATRON
THORN SECURITY

SPONSORS OF THE NEW KOP
BREW XI
BEST BITTER

TILTON ROAD STAND SPONSOR
THE SUITE Factory

TODAY'S MATCH SPONSOR
IMI Precision Diecastings

CLUB SPONSOR
Auto Windscreens

v e r s u s

D E R B Y   C O U N T Y
T U E S D A Y
21st NOVEMBER 1995
K I C K   O F F   7 . 3 0 p m
E n d s l e i g h   L e a g u e
D i v i s i o n   O n e

B I R M I N G H A M
C I T Y Football Club

Endsleigh League

O F F I C I A L   M A T C H D A Y   M A G A Z I N E   price £1.50

yards and pointed to where he wanted the ball played. Derby's captain duly obliged by splitting the Birmingham defence as Sturridge ran in from the left edge of the penalty area behind the defence. As Bennett ran out, the attacker nudged it past him into the goalkeeper's bottom-left-hand corner and celebrated in front off the Derby fans.

The Blues had their fair share of possession and created some half-chances, but Russell Hoult, a day before his 23rd birthday, was equal to anything they could throw at him. On the whole they withstood the pressure from a team unbeaten for so long very well.

It was the van der Laan and Sturridge combination that created the second goal on 39 minutes. Van der Laan's ball downfield was headed clear by Michael Johnson, but only back to the Derby player out on the right touch line. He played the ball forwards and Johnson mis-timed his jump and the ball skidded off the top of his head to Sturridge. Sturridge was away behind the defence, but not in a central position to be able to shoot himself. As he approached the goal area and defenders closing in on him, he squared the ball to an unmarked Willems to turn it neatly into the empty net.

Just as the 45 minutes had been completed, Derby gave away an unnecessary penalty and the opportunity for Birmingham to go in with their tails up.

A ball in from the left-back Cooper saw Gary Rowett bundle into the back of Steve Claridge in an unnecessarily rough challenge, and the referee had no hesitation in giving the penalty-kick. Mark Ward's penalty was hit low to Russell Hoult's left and, despite the 'keeper diving the right way, he was unable to get near it.

Just after the penalty, Gabbiadini had another opportunity to restore the lead as he chased Chris Boden's (who was playing in what was to be his penultimate game for Derby) pass, cut inside and was inches wide with his attempt on goal. One of the potential Birmingham dangerman, Ricky Otto, was being kept quiet by the excellent Lee Carsley.

Just a couple of minutes into the second half, Powell picked up the ball in the middle of the Derby half and

Carsley, Gabbiadini, Sturridge and Yates celebrate another Rams goal.

played a superb ball out to the left wing where Sturridge was waiting. As usual, he ran at pace against the defence and looking up, chipped a cross to the far post where Gabbiadini had pulled back from Michael Johnson. He headed the ball back over the goalkeeper and in off the far post. It was a superb goal all round and restored the two-goal advantage and killed the immediate Birmingham onslaught.

On 73 minutes, Derby scored their fourth goal. A Carsley free-kick was only partially cleared, and a combination of Gary Rowett and Marco Gabbiadini managed to play the ball into the area to Daryll Powell. An excellent piece of skill from the midfielder saw him take one touch which took him clear of the defence and then an excellent shot that, despite a deflection from Bennett's body, that flew into the net.

Russell Hoult was still involved in the game, having to make one save with his legs from a Ken Charlery shot and another near the end of the game when he pulled off a flying save from Claridge. However much The Blues tried to create a clear shot on goal, there always seemed to be a Derby body getting in the way, and the feeling was that Derby were likely to create more chances.

There were a couple of unnecessary bookings for Russell Hoult and Igor Stimac, both for time-wasting, with the score beyond the reach of the home team.

In the end, Derby were better than their West Midlands opponents in every department – Hoult dominated his penalty area, the defence kept the free-scoring forwards quiet, Derby's central midfield pair of van der Laan and Powell were on top form and the forwards showed plenty of pace and movement to worry any defence in the League.

The newly instilled confidence gained by the three successive victories saw them climb the table and embark on a run of 20 unbeaten League games, which took them to the top of the table and within touching distance of promotion. Barry Fry admitted as much. 'We were beaten by a better side,' said the Blues manager. 'They were in charge from start to finish.' It ended a long wait and not many in the crowd will have seen Derby's last victory there, in October 1948 when a Billy Steel goal separated the teams.

This was Derby's best 90 minutes since they beat Middlesbrough 4–2 at Ayresome Park last March, and plenty had changed since then with a substantially new team and change of management and coach.

Jim Smith said that 'overall it was the best performance of the season. We came out and scored a great goal in the first minutes of the second half and then absolutely destroyed Birmingham.'

A big influence in the recent success was the form of Dean Sturridge who had been out injured for 10 weeks, so he was very fresh and full of confidence. Jim Smith suggested some reasons for the change of form '...the system suits the players we have

(Gabbiadini and Sturridge up front with Willems playing behind them and Stimac as a sweeper) rather than playing, as before, with a winger.'

Jimmy Greaves said on television after the game that it was 'the best game of football we have seen so far this season.'

DEAN STURRIDGE

Born: 26 July 1973

First game v Southend United (away), Division Two, 11 January 1992 lost 0–1

Last game v Southampton (away), Premier League, 30 December 2000, lost 0–1

First goal v Millwall (away), Division One, 27 August 1994, lost 1–4

Bought from: –

Sold to: Leicester City

Total appearances: 161 + 53 subs, 58 goals

Consecutive games: 22 from 5 April 1998 to 31 October 1998

Sturridge comes from a footballing family (his brother Simon was a professional at Stoke City and his nephew Daniel is currently with Chelsea) and progressed through the youth team and reserves at Derby. After a successful loan spell at Torquay United (that saw Paul Trollope coming the opposite way) in 1994–95 he was eventually given his chance when Jim Smith arrived as manager.

As first-choice striker, his pace and shooting always caused problems for defences, and during the promotion season he was top scorer with 20 goals. The following season he scored 11 goals, including a goal of the season contender at Highbury against Arsenal. There was transfer speculation surrounding a £7 million fee, but Derby wanted to keep him and missed the chance of cashing in on his success.

He remains Derby's record scorer in the Premier League and he was eventually sold to Leicester City for a modest fee of £375,000 in January 2001.

DERBY COUNTY 2
CRYSTAL PALACE 1

Division One   **Sunday 28 April 1996**

Baseball Ground

Derby County: Hoult, Rowett, C Powell, Trollope, Carbon, Stimac, van der Laan, Sturridge, Simpson (Ward 83), Gabbiadini (Willems 63), Flynn. Other sub: Carsley.

Crystal Palace: Martyn, Edworthy, Brown, Roberts, Anderson (Ndah 72), Hopkin, Pitcher, Houghton, Freedman (Veart 89), Dyer (Vincent 79), Rodger.

Referee: D.B. Allison (Lancaster)

Attendance: 17,041

Coming into this game, Sunderland were already promoted on 83 points, Derby were second on 76 and Crystal Palace on 75. This meant that, with just one game remaining after this one, a win would seal Derby's promotion to the Premier League for the first time. Derby's last game would be a potentially awkward away game at West Bromwich Albion, while Palace had a relatively easy-looking home game against Norwich City, so winning this game would put the matter beyond doubt. A draw meant that the Londoners would be favourites for promotion going into the last weekend of the regular season, and the losers would go into the Play-offs.

The publicity machine had been working overtime in the build up to the game, with a near capacity crowd expected, with the slogan 'Roar 'til you're Raw' being prominent and fans encouraged to wear black and white for the afternoon, as the Baseball Ground hosted the live TV game.

Derby's team selection was thrown into confusion on the morning of the game as the new Player of the Year, Dean Yates, failed to recover from a knee injury picked up in training during the week, and his place went to Matt Carbon who was signed from Lincoln City on transfer deadline day. Carbon had had a busy week – the previous weekend he missed a last-minute header in the draw with

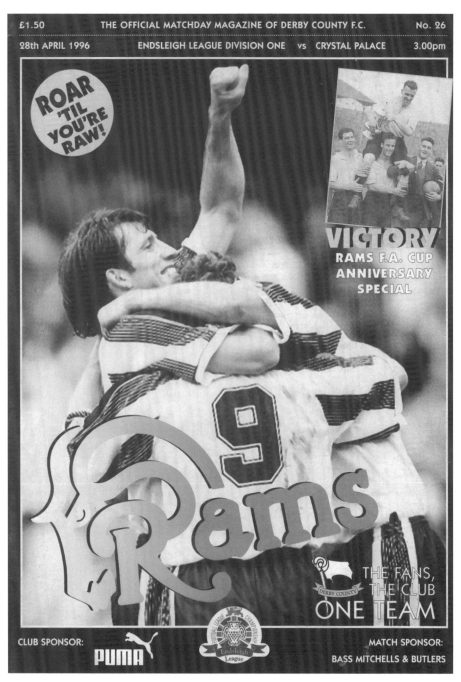

Birmingham City when it seemed easier to score, which would have made the Palace game so much easier. He then came on to play as a second-half substitute to make his debut for the England Under-21 team in their game against Croatia at Roker Park, Sunderland.

Dean Yates had made 42 consecutive appearances for Derby and was in tears as the realisation of the failed fitness test sank in and that he would miss such an important game. Jim Smith had the option of recalling Darren Wassall into the centre of defence but instead decided on the 20-year-old Carbon for his first full game.

Igor Stimac was also away during the week with the Croatia national team and played for a large part of the game against England at Wembley, before being substituted with one eye on the important club fixtures at this crucial stage of the season.

Other team changes from the previous week's 1–1 draw with Birmingham City were the inclusion of Sean Flynn in place of Lee Carsley and the forwards Sturridge (returning from suspension) and Gabbiadini coming in for Ashley Ward and Ron Willems, who dropped to the bench. Ward, another transfer deadline day signing, was clearly not fully fit and struggled in these final matches of the season.

Palace had been relegated from the Premier League at the end of the previous season and lost many of their star players. Dave Bassett was appointed as their new manger only three months prior to this match. At that time they were in 16th place and since then had gone on an impressive run taking them up to third place.

Indeed, Palace were going for a new club record of five successive away wins, having equalled their record with the recent 2–0 win at Wolverhampton Wanderers. They changed their formation a little, reverting to a regular 4–4–2 formation instead of playing the three centre halves as they had been doing.

The game was broadcast live on ITV, and had been moved to the Sunday afternoon game, but there was still a near capacity crowd and a good travelling support from South London. Derby got off to the best possible start, playing towards the Normanton End in the first half. With just two minutes played, Simpson controlled a clearance from Stimac on his chest and, as he turned, played a good ball between the defenders, and this allowed Sturridge to outpace them both and rush forwards unchallenged. He took one touch of the ball before he then curled the ball into Nigel Martyn's bottom-left-hand corner to score his 19th goal of the season. In such an important game, scoring so early on meant an awfully long time to hang on and plenty of time for nerves to play a part, not only from the players but from the stands as well.

Within a couple of minutes, Palace were on level terms when Dyer beat Sean Flynn and pulled the ball back to the penalty area, where Kenny Brown, on loan from West Ham United, scored with a superb volley past Russell Hoult, much to the delight of the travelling fans.

This goal seemed to rattle Derby, and Palace settled much better for the next 30 minutes and passed the ball around with some confidence, but significantly they did not force Hoult into any serious saves and take advantage while they were on top. Derby's play, however, was scrappy, with passes going astray regularly.

Sturridge might have added a second, when van der Laan's fine pass put him clear again, but Martyn was able to smother the shot this time.

At half-time, with the score at 1–1, the general feeling was that Derby had played themselves out of the sticky spell and that Palace had probably missed their opportunity to win this game. However, it was still all to play for with the scores level and with Derby knowing that within 45 minutes they could be in the Premier League, but they had to score otherwise the season would hang on the last game.

Arguably the most important 45 minutes of the decade started in controversial manner when Sturridge went down in the penalty area following a challenge by Leif Andersen. The referee, however, was not impressed and waved away all appeals.

Gabbiadini had been dropped for the last game because he had not been scoring goals on a regular basis and again appeared to be struggling to create an end product. Jim Smith decided to change things around just after the hour mark and brought on the Dutchman Ron Willems, who had missed some recent games through injury.

Immediately this change brought about Derby's second goal. Willems won a corner off Ray Houghton.

The corner was taken from the 'Catcher's Corner' (a reference back to the days when the ground was used for baseball) between the Ley Stand and Osmaston Road Stand by Paul Simpson. He swung the ball to the far post where Robbie van der Laan had taken a couple of steps back from his marker and was able to jump unmarked and unchallenged and headed the ball down and past Nigel Martyn, sparking scenes of jubilation around the old stadium.

Van der Laan explained afterwards that the players had been practicing the move on the training ground during the week, but had not worked so well – probably as he was not expecting to have so much time and space. The confidence that Derby lacked for the last 30 minutes of the first half suddenly returned and Palace did not look to have the ability or desire to force another equaliser.

Palace were now at the stage of throwing everything at Derby and replaced defender Andersen with forward George Ndah with 20 minutes to play.

It was a nerve-wracking last few minutes that passed without incident. Referee Allison finally blew for full-time, sparking scenes of jubilation around the Baseball Ground, from fans to players to the Directors' Box.

It had been a remarkable season, not least because when Jim Smith arrived there were several senior players who were out of contract and left (Pembridge, Williams, Short), and his new squad and new coach (Steve McClaren) struggled to get established for the first third of the season. The signing of Igor Stimac was key and set the club off on a run of 20 games unbeaten which propelled them to the top of the table. Despite a wobble following a defeat at the eventual champions Sunderland they achieved more than anyone had hoped for.

The aim now was to create a squad capable of remaining in the Premier League and, like Sunderland, were one year away from moving into a new, purpose-built stadium.

Palace reached the Play-off Final, defeating Charlton Athletic in their semi-final, but lost to Leicester City 2–1 in the Final to a Steve Claridge goal in extra-time.

ROBIN VAN DER LAAN

Born: 5 September 1968
Debut v Port Vale (home), Division One, 13 August 1995, draw 0–0
Last game v Southampton (away), Premier League, 2 May 1998, lost 2–0
First goal v Portsmouth (away), Division One, 16 September 1995, draw 2–2
Bought from: Port Vale
Sold to: Barnsley
Total appearances: 70 + 7 subs, 11 goals
Consecutive appearances: 23 from 13 August 1995 to 2 December 1995

Dutchman van der Laan had five years playing for Port Vale, where he was originally signed as a striker, and jumped at the chance in the summer of 1995 to move down the A50 to become Jim Smith's captain for a fee of £475,000. The transfer also involved striker Lee Mills going in the opposite direction, something of a surprise as Mills had only been at Derby since February and had scored seven goals in his 16 appearances.

Robbie was the driving force in midfield and scored the all-important promotion-winning goal against Crystal Palace. He was allowed to go to Wolverhampton Wanderers on loan for a period in the 1996–97 season but became an important figure in the second half of the season to help maintain Premier League status.

He was sold to Barnsley at the start of the 1998–99 season for £325,000 and remained there until a knee injury forced him to retire in 2001.

DERBY COUNTY 3
LEEDS UNITED 3

Premier League   **Saturday 17 August 1996**

Baseball Ground

Derby County: Hoult, Yates, Laursen (Flynn, 75), Rowett, Parker, Dailly, D. Powell (Simpson, 75), C. Powell, Asanovic, Sturridge, Gabbiadini (Willems, 75). Other subs: van der Laan, Taylor (gk).

Leeds United: Martyn, Jobson, Palmer, Radebe (Wetherall, 88), Kelly, Ford, Bowyer, Couzens (Tinkler, 85), Sharpe, Rush, Deane (Harte, 57). Other subs: Wallace, Beeney (gk).

Referee: P.S. Danson (Leicester)

Attendance: 17,927

Following their promotion, the hype and expectation of the first season in the Premier League was great and Derby were not given a kind start, with the first four fixtures against Leeds United (home), Tottenham Hotspur (away), Aston Villa (away) and Manchester United (home) – 'a pretty horrendous start' said Jim Smith in recognition of the fact that these were the type of games that the club wanted to be involved with.

Jim Smith was keen to get going, but also with a hint of apprehension as he said he always looks forward to the first Saturday but it had come around all too quickly.

'I'm a bit disappointed that so many people in the media seem to have written us off already. Nothing will give us greater pleasure than to prove the so-called experts wrong – by a long way'. Elsewhere in the Premier League, former Derby favourite Bruce Rioch had been sacked by Arsenal before the season even started in a dispute over transfer funds.

As usual the season kicked-off on a very warm

The Ram

Derby County
v Leeds United

Saturday August 17th 1996
Kick-Off 3.00pm

Issue No.1

The Croatian
Connection: What
Igor said to
the gaffer
about Ace
Asanovic

EXCLUSIVE

Dailly date
with
destiny:
Why I
chose the
Rams

Match sponsor: BASS

PUMA
CLUB SPONSOR

F.A. CARLING PREMIERSHIP

THE OFFICIAL DERBY COUNTY MATCHDAY MAGAZINE   £1.50

and sunny August afternoon in front of a near-capacity crowd. One regret that Derby
would have had is that the planned redevelopment of the Baseball Ground had not already
been completed as they entered the Premier League with a capacity of around 18000 with
the distinct possibility that every game would be an all-ticket game and sell-out.

Derby welcomed three new arrivals into the starting line-up – Jacob Laursen, Christian Dailly and Aljosa Asanovic (signed before the Euro '96 Championships on a recommendation by his friend Igor Stimac).

Leeds had recruited a number of players during the summer costing several million pounds. The more high-profile ones being Nigel Martyn (£2.25 million from Crystal Palace), Lee Sharpe (£4.5 million from Manchester United) and Lee Bowyer (£2.6 million from Charlton Athletic). Ian Rush also joined them on a free transfer from Liverpool.

Derby's preparations had been hampered during the build up to the big kick-off – Daryll Powell had a bout of chicken pox, Igor Stimac had a back spasm, Matt Carbon (Achilles), Ashley Ward (double hernia) and Robbie van der Laan (ankle) also carrying knocks. Without kicking a ball in the new season, Derby's resources were already stretched.

With Stimac missing, Jacob Laursen, who had been away during the week on international duty for Denmark, would line-up in the centre of the defence and Paul Parker would come in at right-back. Parker had just been released by Manchester United, having been displaced in the team by a young Gary Neville, and was brought in on a short-term contract and found himself playing in this historic first game in the Premier League. In Stimac's absence, Dean Yates had the honour of being Derby's first captain in the Premier League.

It took just 18 minutes for a Derby player to score in the Premier League – unfortunately, it was an own goal!. Leeds were attacking towards the Osmaston End and their fans saw them move the ball from right to left with new boys Sharpe and Bowyer involved. Bowyer hit a diagonal low cross into the Derby area and there looked to be no danger with Hoult preparing to make a save. Laursen tried to block the ball but only succeeded in deflecting it into his own net with Hoult out of position. Not the start the Dane would have liked on his first appearance in English football.

Derby were not being outplayed and had two good chances as the game approached the interval. A free-kick taken short to Chris Powell allowed him to deliver a deep cross to the far post. Everyone missed it and the ball fell to Dean Yates who was unmarked on the corner of the goal area. His angled shot missed the far post by inches. Derby's best move of the game saw them move the ball from one side of the field to another in superb fashion, with pace and skill. Marco Gabbiadini and Daryll Powell combined in Derby's half to win the ball and Powell played a superb ball inside the Leeds defenders and set Sturridge off down the left wing in front of the Popside. He flicked the ball across with the outside of his right foot and both Dailly and Gabbiadini, who had raced downfield, slid in but could not get any contact to the ball.

The half-time team talk would have been to keep Derby playing football as they were not getting outplayed and opportunities were being, and would be created.

Brian Deane was replaced by Ian Harte following a strong, but fair challenge from Yates and the substitute was soon involved. Jumping with Chris Powell on halfway he nodded the ball down to Bowyer who was allowed to run towards the penalty area. Harte continued his run forward unmarked and when Bowyer squared the ball to him 25 yards out, he hit a strong low shot past Hoult into the bottom right hand corner of the net.

That goal saw Derby make all their three substitutions in one go with 15 minutes remaining. Sean Flynn, Paul Simpson and Ron Willems came on for their Premiership debuts replacing Laursen, Daryll Powell and Gabbiadini. Within three minutes the changes produced results. Gary Rowett launched a ball forward from the halfway line, Christian Dailly flicked the ball on, beating Radebe and it came to Sturridge on the edge of the area. A magnificent piece of skill, initially controlling with his right foot and turning at the same time and as the ball dropped hit an unstoppable left foot volley beyond Martyn.

With the ground still cheering, Leeds restarted the game and worked the ball backwards, Rush to Bowyer to Jobson (who started his career at Burton Albion in the Northern Premier League). His attempted backpass to Martyn was underhit allowing Paul Simpson to follow it and as Simpson and the goalkeeper went into a tackle just outside the penalty area, the ball broke nicely for Derby and bobbled into an unguarded net. The goal time was actually just nine seconds from Leeds kicking off until the goal and turned the game around from 2–0 down to 2–2 in a very short space of time.

At this point it may have been wise to sit back, calm down and settle for the draw, but as we have read elsewhere it is very difficult not to get caught up in the atmosphere. As Leeds were stunned by being pegged back so suddenly Derby created another good chance – Dean Yates again getting on the end of a Gary Rowett corner, and his downward header beat everyone and unfortunately hit the underside of the bar before being cleared.

Leeds duly went up to the Normanton End and scored their third goal – a deep Harte cross was flicked on by Bowyer and nodded down by Rush into the path of the now unmarked Bowyer who scored with ease. There was a hint of offside, but Dailly and Yates were caught ball watching as Bowyer ran past them.

One last spell of Derby pressure was rewarded as the game moved towards the last minute. An Asanovic cross was drilled between three defenders down by the 'C' Stand corner that was booted clear by Radebe, only for Rowett to return the ball forwards from halfway. Radebe let the ball bounce past him 18 yards from goal and found

Sturridge who was goal side of him. The striker hit the ball first time along the floor leaving Martyn stranded. It was 3–3 and an unbelievable last 15 minutes since the introduction of the substitutes. At that point, with five minutes of injury time to play on a very hot afternoon, both teams settled for a draw.

It was an exciting first taste of the Premier League, and it was clearly evident that the standard of play was a lot better than the second tier, and defenders would not be able to give teams any opportunities to score as the strikers were far more clinical in their finishing.

Generally speaking, scoring three goals in any game, especially in a Premier League, should be enough to take the points and as such both managers would be left with some work to do. In terms of defence, Derby knew they could not get away with slack marking at this level, and they would have to learn quickly as this fixture against Leeds United was probably the easiest of the opening four games.

PAUL SIMPSON

Born: 26 July 1966
Debut v Leicester City (away), Division Two, 22 February 1992, won 2–1
Last game v Southend United (home), League Cup, 1 October 1997, won 5–0

First goal v Leicester City (away), Division Two, 22 February 1992, won 2–1
Bought from: Oxford United
Sold to: Wolverhampton Wanderers
Total appearances: 164 + 61 subs, 57 goals
Consecutive games: 41 from 22 February 1992 to 21 November 1992

Simpson was a skillful left winger or left-sided midfield player with an eye for goal – over 60 goals in 230 appearances before joining Derby. It was this ability that Arthur Cox paid £500,000 to Oxford United for in February 1992.

He became a vital part of the Derby team during this time (he scored four goals in his first five games) and he twice hit more than 10 goals in a season. Jim Smith used him in nearly all of the Division Two promotion season games, but half of those appearances were as substitute. He was used even less in the Premier League, with just 19 substitute appearances, but is best remembered for his two goals in the opening day draw against Leeds United.

With the influx of new attacking players, Simpson's opportunities were decreasing and he joined Wolverhampton Wanderers in October 1997, initially on loan, then permanently for a fee of £75,000.

DERBY COUNTY 0
MIDDLESBROUGH 2

FA Cup sixth round   **Saturday 8 March 1997**

Baseball Ground

Derby County: Taylor, Carsley, Dailly, Stimac, C. Powell, Flynn (Rowett, 45), D. Powell (Simpson, 72), Trollope, Asanovic: Willems (Gabbiadini, 83), Ward.
Middlesbrough: Roberts, Fleming, Pearson, Festa, Blackmore, Hignett, Stamp, Mustoe, Juninho, Ravanelli, Beck. Subs: Cox, Vickers, Moore.
Referee: Graham Poll (Tring)
Attendance: 17,567

Derby had overcome Gillingham (after an abandoned first game), Aston Villa and Coventry City to reach the sixth round of the FA Cup competition and Middlesbrough had beaten Chester (6–0 at home), Hednesford Town (3–2 away) and Manchester City (1–0 away).

After 102 years of staging FA Cup ties at the Baseball Ground, this one was to be the last with the impending move to Pride Park to take place during the summer months, and a semi-final place up for grabs. As a rearranged Premier League fixture, the two teams met at the Riverside just three days previously where Derby's defence completely fell to pieces in the last half an hour as Middlesbrough ran out 6–1 winners, including three goals in a five-minute spell. Jim Smith was left with many problems to deal with – injuries, suspensions and loss of form in defence.

That defeat left Derby in 14th place, seven points clear of the relegation zone with nine games left to play. Middlesbrough,

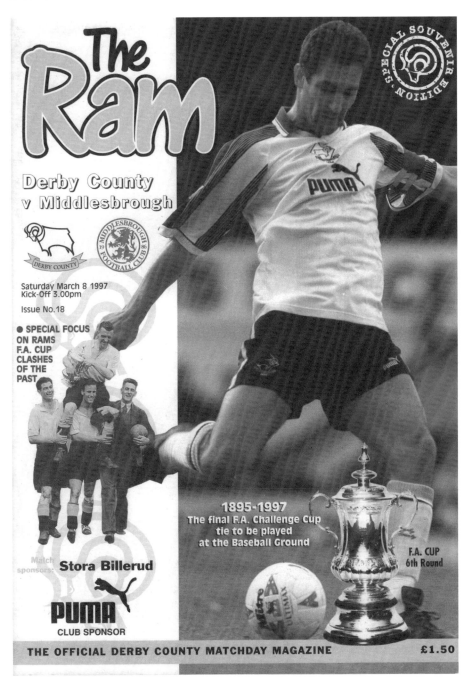

The Ram

Derby County v Middlesbrough

Saturday March 8 1997
Kick-Off 3.00pm

Issue No.18

● SPECIAL FOCUS ON RAMS F.A. CUP CLASHES OF THE PAST

SPECIAL SOUVENIR EDITION

1895-1997
The final F.A. Challenge Cup tie to be played at the Baseball Ground

F.A. CUP
6th Round

Match sponsors: Stora Billerud

PUMA
CLUB SPONSOR

THE OFFICIAL DERBY COUNTY MATCHDAY MAGAZINE   £1.50

despite the midweek win, were sitting bottom of the table, 10 points behind the safety zone, and they had had three points deducted (which ultimately lost them their Premier League place) for failing to play a fixture at Blackburn Rovers due to the claimed illness of 23 members of the squad.

Middlesbrough had spent several millions of pounds on expensive foreign players such as Emerson, Juninho, Ravanelli and Festa, and Ravanelli's goals had helped them reach the League Cup Final, where they were to lose to Leicester City after a replay. This multi-million pound investment in players meant Middlesbrough could score plenty of goals, but the defence was always liable to concede more.

Middlesbrough were forced into changing their goalkeeper for the game – Mark Schwarzer was Cup tied having played for Bradford City in the early rounds and was replaced by Roberts and Emerson and Kinder replaced by Stamp and Blackmore respectively.

Jim Smith, in his programme notes, said '…it's not often you have the opportunity to restore pride in a matter of days against a team that has just turned you over'.

Smith made five changes from the midweek team – Jacob Laursen was injured in the defeat at the Riverside (and sparked the defensive collapse when he went off) and was replaced by Paul Trollope who was returning from suspension; Marco Gabbiadini returned from a month's loan at Oxford United and took a place on the bench; Dean Sturridge was starting a two-match ban after reaching 21 points and replaced by Ron Willems; Russel Hoult appeared to have lost a bit of confidence and so Martin Taylor was brought into the starting line up; Robbie van der Laan failed a late fitness test and was replaced by Sean Flynn and Daryll Powell came in for Gary Rowett, who passed a fitness test but was not 100 per cent so was named as a substitute. Paul McGrath was still out injured. This was Martin Taylor's first start for nearly two and a half years since suffering a horrendous broken leg injury as a result of a challenge by Southend United striker Dave Regis, and it had been a long and painful return to action.

Jim Smith was forced into a change of formation – reverting to a back four instead of the three centre-halves that they had been utilising. The loss of van der Laan and Sturridge, both crucial to the Derby team, made the team look under strength and put the focal point on Asanovic to control the game.

Derby started the game with Daryll Powell and Lee Carsley hustling their Boro counterparts and tackling strongly in midfield, although the first two chances went to the visitors, with Martin Taylor getting early opportunities to get involved and get rid of any lingering nerves. Firstly, he turned round a shot from Beck and then blocked a Ravanelli shot from the resulting corner.

Paul Trollope had Derby's first effort on goal when his 25-yard shot was narrowly wide of the post. Curtis Fleming was given the job of man-marking Asanovic, and this close attention of Derby's main threat limited his influence on the game. It was not all done fairly, with a great deal of pushing, shoving and elbows as they went for every ball together.

Middlesbrough were creating more frequent and better opportunities, with Juninho being at the heart of all their good moves. After one good move that allowed a Juninho shot which Taylor saved, the little Brazilian was not to be denied and on 39 minutes he played a one-two with Hignett, ran into the box, and cleverly chipped the ball over Martin Taylor as he rushed out. Even from this point, with the game pattern as it had been, it was difficult to see how Derby could get back into the game other than from a mistake or a set piece move.

Half-time allowed Derby to re-organise, as the current tactics were clearly not working. Gary Rowett replaced Sean Flynn and a change of formation saw the usual back three formation return, commanded by Igor Stimac, with Trollope told to stick with Juninho. This was to stop Middlesbrough's creativity, but it did not address Derby's problem at the other end – a lack of firepower, as they were missing the pace of Dean Sturridge.

When Derby did have a chance from a set piece, Middlesbrough's stand-in goalkeeper was up to the task, pushing round an Asanovic free-kick and Trollope fired a shot over the angle of post and bar.

As the game progressed in the second half and Derby's midfield were throttled, the long, high ball launched forward became the norm. This played into the hands of the Middlesbrough defence where Nigel Pearson and Gianluca Festa (signed from Inter Milan) were able to easily beat Ward and Willems, who were getting all too predictable.

At the other end, Mikkel Beck had two opportunities to put the game beyond Derby, both saved by Martin Taylor – the first when he spread himself and the second by clearing the ball outside the area. Derby had to push forward to try and get an equaliser, but the final pass would never be quite right. This left gaps at the back and as the game moved towards injury-time, Middlesbrough broke away, and inevitably it was Juninho that played a clever ball into Ravanelli, whose left foot shot flew into the net for his 25th goal of the season.

Overall, Middlesbrough were the better team on the day and Juninho was the main difference, being the most inventive player on the field and saw them beat Derby for the second time in four days. Man of the Match was Martin Taylor, and that says it all about the disappointing performance, which was down to a lack of strength in depth and the combination of crucial players missing and too many others having a poor game (Dailly, Powell, Flynn and Willems). The one proven goalscorer on the bench, Marco Gabbiadini, was introduced with just six minutes to play and too late to have any impact.

From Derby's point of view, this was probably the best opportunity of reaching the FA Cup Final in many years, with the winners of this game being drawn to play fellow

Derbyshire team Chesterfield at Old Trafford. An all-Derbyshire semi-final would have been most unlikely and unique, but not to be on this occasion. Middlesbrough required a replay at Hillsborough to get past Chesterfield, the first game ending 3–3 after extra time when they were winning 2–0 after an hour. Derby's attention could now be concentrated on maintaining their Premier League status, with three more wins needed to guarantee it.

Martin Taylor was to make just three more appearances for Derby before the signing of Mart Poom, who came in as the goalkeeper to challenge Russell Hoult.

Middlesbrough, never having reached a Cup Final in their history, were to reach the League Cup and FA Cup Finals in the same season. Their Cup Final experience was not one to remember as they lost 2–0 to Chelsea, with Roberto di Matteo scoring one of the fastest Cup Final goals ever, after just 42 seconds.

MARTIN TAYLOR

Born: 9 December 1966
Debut v West Ham United (home), League Cup, 24 January 1990, draw 0–0
Last game v Nottingham Forest (home), Premier League, 23 April 1997, draw 0–0
Bought from: Mile Oak Rovers
Sold to: Wycombe Wanderers
Total appearances: 120
Consecutive games: 92 from 10 February 1993 to 1 October 1994

Taylor's potential was spotted early and he was brought in as under-study to Peter Shilton. To gain valuable League experience, he spent time on loan at several other lower League clubs (Carlisle United, Scunthorpe United, Crewe Alexandra and Wycombe Wanderers) until Shilton left. The gloves changed hands between Taylor and Steve Sutton until Taylor established himself and took the Player of the Year for the 1993–94 season. An horrendous double leg break at Southend United in October 1994 put him out of action for nearly two and a half years. By the time he returned, Hoult was ahead of him and Derby then brought in Mart Poom as well, potentially making him third choice. He was not offered a new contract at the end of the 1996–97 season and, following his testimonial game (the last official game at the Baseball Ground), he left for Wycombe Wanderers, where he was a fan favourite and reached an FA Cup semi-final.

MANCHESTER UNITED 2
DERBY COUNTY 3

PREMIER LEAGUE   **SATURDAY 5 APRIL 1997**

OLD TRAFFORD

Manchester United: Schmeichel, G. Neville (Irwin, 70), Johnsen, Pallister (Scholes, 86), P. Neville, Beckham, Keane, Butt (Solskjaer, 45), Giggs, Cantona, Cole. Other subs: Poborsky, Van der Gouw (gk).

Derby County: Poom, Laursen, McGrath, Dailly, C. Powell, Trollope, van der Laan, D. Powell, Wanchope (Simpson, 66), Ward, Sturridge. Other subs: Hoult (gk), Willems, Carbon, Solis.

Referee: D.R. Elleray (Harrow)

Attendance: 55,243

Derby surprisingly gave debuts to Mart Poom and Paulo Wanchope, with his Costa Rican compatriot named as one of the substitutes. The Costa Rican pair were signed in a combined deal worth £1.25 million, but manager Jim Smith sprang a transfer deadline surprise with the £500,000 signing of Poom from Estonia, where he was the international goalkeeper. Other movements on transfer deadline day were all outbound loan deals for Darren Wassall (Birmingham City), Sean Flynn (Stoke City) and Kevin Cooper (Stockport County).

Manchester United were the current Premier League champions and had won 11 of the 15 home League games, conceding just 11 goals. Derby's away form was not so good in their first Premier League season – just one win and seven draws from the 16 games played so far. After the Derby game, United were to be away at Borussia Dortmund on the following Wednesday in the first leg of the semi-finals of the European Cup.

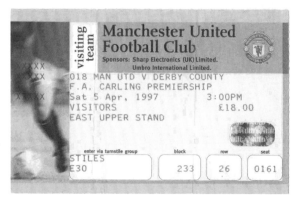

FA Carling Premiership
Derby County
Kick Off 3.00pm

SEASON
1996-97

OFFICIAL

Saturday 5th April 1997
£1.50
Volume 58, No.20

PROGRAMME

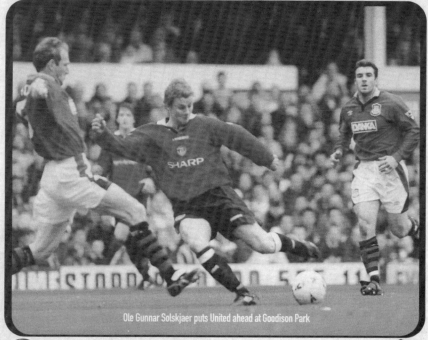

Ole Gunnar Solskjaer puts United ahead at Goodison Park

Official Club Sponsor
SHARP

Official kit & ball supplier

Derby had lost their last three away games, conceding 11 goals, and had won one of the last four games. United had lost two of the last 23 games. United were sitting top of the League, six points clear of Arsenal and Liverpool, and Derby were in 14th place, five points clear of the bottom three which were currently Coventry City, Nottingham Forest and Southampton, with seven games of the season to play.

Paul Trollope was given the unenviable job of man-marking Eric Cantona and Paul McGrath made his first return to Old Trafford in a Derby shirt, after being released by Aston Villa.

Derby were kicking towards the Stretford End in the first half and showed no nerves playing at the Old Trafford stadium or by the large attendance.

Ashley Ward won a header and followed up his own flick-on near the left edge of the United penalty area. As support arrived he laid the ball back to Chris Powell who had come forward from the back, and he played it to Paul Trollope in the middle of the field. Trollope knocked the ball to the far post where Wanchope out-jumped Phil Neville and the ball fell to Ward, who had run into the penalty area. Ward slightly mis-timed his shot under pressure form Johnsen and hit the ball into the ground. The ball bounced and looped over Peter Schmeichel into the net to give Derby a well-deserved lead.

Things were to get much better for Derby when the unknown debutant from Cost Rica became an overnight sensation and wrote his name in Derby history forever. Daryll Powell won the ball off Roy Keane mid way in the Derby half and passed the ball out to the right, still some 10 yards in his own half, where Wanchope was in space.

Jim Smith often commented about Wanchope that the player did not know what he was going to do next with the ball, so his teammates had no chance.

Wanchope just started running with the ball, at pace towards the United goal at the Stretford End, still controlling the ball. Not one of the United defenders could get near enough to him to make a tackle. These were not just any defenders he was playing against, but international players, playing in the best League in the world.

Sturridge made an intelligent run across the penalty area and that also distracted the covering players, but by then Wanchope was approaching the edge of the penalty area and as he was surrounded by four United defenders, and faced with the world's best goalkeeper it still seemed unlikely that he would get a shot in and beat Schmeichel. His long right leg managed to get in a shot into the bottom-left corner of the net and beat Schmeichel. A remarkable goal which gave Derby a 2–0 lead that they could hardly have planned for at kick-off.

In truth, the scoreline did not flatter Derby at all, and they could have gone in at half-time with an even better scoreline, but for two chances spurned by Ashley Ward when he really should have done better. Jim Smith in a later interview still could not believe what was happening. 'I've never been in a situation where I was 2–0 up at Old Trafford at half-time'. He had a strange mix of emotions – extremely happy at being 2–0 up; equally as angry that with a bit more clinical finishing and composure in front of goal it could have been 4–0; full of dread at the United attacking onslaught that would surely be coming in the second half. Even at this stage, Smith was still thinking no further than getting a draw, which would still have been an achievement.

As with any game, the third goal would be very important. If United were to score then the impetus would be in their favour and if Derby scored, the points should be theirs. Alex Ferguson's response at half-time, other than being extremely upset, was to replace Nicky Butt in the midfield with an extra forward in Solskjaer.

Within minutes of the re-start the pattern for the half was already established, with United having to attack and Derby's attacks being limited to the occasional counter attacks and breaks up field, utilising the pace of Sturridge and unpredictability of Wanchope.

What Derby wanted to avoid was giving United an early goal in the second half as that would just mean United would apply constant pressure. Unfortunately for Derby, that is what happened. Paul Trollope, who had been brought into the team to mark Cantona, lost him as a cross came towards the penalty area in a central position, and one touch and a shot later the score was 2–1.

It was from one of the rare counter attacks that Derby restored their two-goal advantage with a goal from Dean Sturridge, with some assistance from the United defence. There was no great build up to the goal, but Sturridge's determination to chase every ball got his reward. A long goal-kick from Poom went beyond Ward and when the ball came to Gary Pallister, under pressure form Sturridge, he could only slice a clearance towards his own goal.

Sturridge chased with Pallister after the ball and Schmeichel came charging out of his area as well to cover the ball. As the ball bounced, Sturridge jumped first, with neither the goalkeeper (unable to use his hands at this point) or defender making a definite decision. As the ball bounced towards the net, Johnsen was the covering defender but as he approached the ball to hack clear, he slipped and ended in the net himself. The ball, however, hit the post and bounced up nicely for Sturridge to tap into an empty net from two yards before wheeling away to the Derby fans in the corner.

Jim Smith later admitted that even with the score at 3–1, he was still only thinking of a draw as he thought United would have too much midfield strength and forward firepower to keep them quiet for the remainder of the game.

Inevitably, United managed to create chances and eventually found a way through the Derby defence. Cantona eventually lost his marker Trollope with some clever footwork and chipped a ball towards the Derby penalty area. The Derby defender, McGrath, could only flick the ball on and it fell into the path of substitute Solskjaer who lashed it, first time, into the net giving Poom no chance.

The last 10 minutes saw United throw everything and everybody (Paul Scholes was brought on as another forward replacing defender Pallister) forward, and this made for an exciting and tense finish, especially for the travelling fans.

The result, even with six games to go (including four home games), went a long way to Derby surviving their first season in the Premier League, but with still some awkward looking games left to play – Newcastle United (away), Arsenal (home) and local rivals Nottingham Forest (home). The recognised survival points target of 40 points was within reach (two points) and unless anything spectacular was to happen among the teams at the bottom of the table, safety was assured.

The attendance was the largest to see Derby play in a League game since the fixture at Old Trafford in 1978 that was watched by 57,115 when United won easily 4–0.

Jim Smith said 'I've never seen a team work so hard in my life. Everyone of them worked tremendously hard'.

It was a match that Wanchope, in particular, and probably the rest of the team will remember forever. Certainly Wanchope's goal will be replayed on a regular basis every time the teams meet, and during Derby's 125th Anniversary celebrations that goal was voted by the fans as Derby's greatest-ever goal. Although the goal was the highlight, it should be remembered that it was also the debut of goalkeeper Mart Poom, who was to become one of Derby's best, and most appreciated goalkeepers. This was certainly the result of the season and probably of the decade.

PAULO WANCHOPE

Born: 31 July 1976
Debut v Manchester United (away), Premier League, 5 April 1997 won 3–2
Last game v Chelsea (away), Premier League, 16 May 1999, lost 1–2
First goal v Manchester United (away), Premier League, 5 April 1997 won 3–2
Bought from: Club Sport Herediano, Costa Rica
Sold to: West Ham United
Total appearances: 75 + 8 subs, 28 goals
Consecutive games: 36, from 14 February 1998 to 28 December 1898

Paulo César Wanchope Watson, originally came with his fellow countryman Mauricio

Solis on trial, having also been to QPR, during the 1996–97 season and played a few reserve-team games. This followed a recommendation from Bob McNab, the former Arsenal full-back in the US.

He was signed for £700,000 and made his impact in his debut at Old Trafford. That goal has been voted as the best Derby goal of all time in the poll conducted as part of the club's 125 Celebrations. His excellent control and pace for a big man made opposition defences worry and his unpredictability on the ball made him a handful, for his own teammates as well. In October 1997 he was named

as the Premier League Player of the Month.

Wanchope is the most prolific goalscorer in the history of the Cost Rica national team (45 goals in 73 games) and in February 1998 scored four goals for them against Cuba.

With his contract having a year left to run, Derby decided to take the £3.5 million offered by West Ham United, rather than risk him leaving for free.

DERBY COUNTY 1
ARSENAL 3

Premier League   **Sunday 11 May 1997**

Baseball Ground

Derby County: Poom, Rowett, McGrath (Carsley, 55), Dailly, Laursen, van der Laan, D. Powell (Trollope, 44), Asanovic, C. Powell, Ward, Willems (Simpson, 76). Other subs: Hoult (gk), Yates.

Arsenal: Seaman, Keown, Adams, Bould, Dixon, Platt, Vieira (Parlour, 76), Merson (Anelka, 7), Winterburn, Bergkamp, Wright. Other subs: Lukic (gk), Marshall, Hughes.

Referee: P.A. Durkin (Portland)

Attendance: 18, 287

Derby had announced, prior to the match against Luton Town in February 1996, that the club would be moving to a new purpose-built stadium on the Pride Park development in time for the start of the 1997–98 season. All of this happened very quickly when the plans to re-develop the existing site at the Baseball Ground had been approved. The Baseball Hotel next to the stadium had been demolished in readiness and dates agreed for the start of the work. The re-building of the existing stadium was a matter of days away when the opportunity to move to Pride Park came about and was grasped with both hands

After 102 years since their first game at the old stadium (v Sunderland in September 1895), a day of celebrations had been organised which included – limited edition programmes, brochures, badges, former players parade by the likes of Alan Hinton, Charlie George, Dave Mackay and a carnival atmosphere all round the ground with the Arsenal fans joining in and respecting the occasion (something they themselves would go through a decade later when they moved from Highbury to the Emirates Stadium).

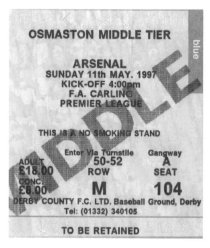

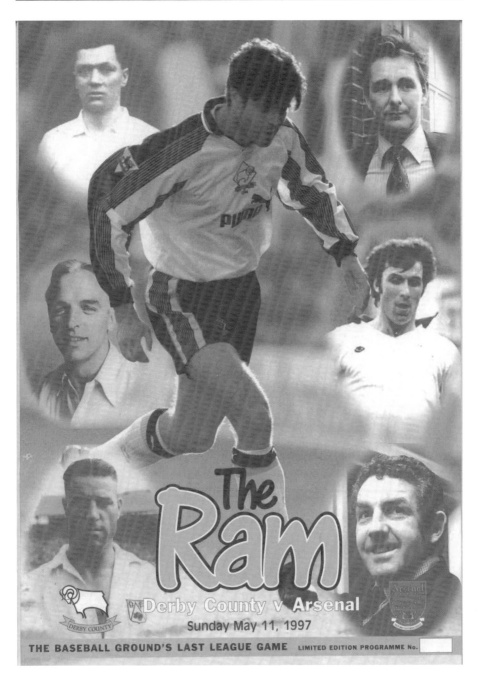

It was always going to be an emotional afternoon, and for many derby fans this would be their last visit to the old ground. Paul McGrath had announced his intention to retire from football due to persistent knee problems, which meant that he was rarely able to train and the Arsenal game would be his last.

There was nothing to play for in the game itself – Derby's place in the Premier League for the following season had been assured a couple of weeks ago and Arsenal were guaranteed a top-four finish regardless of the result. This meant a more relaxed atmosphere and the event could be enjoyed and appreciated as Chris Powell was named as the Player of the Year.

Arsenal came to Derby as one of the leading clubs and had a squad full of international stars – David Seaman, Lee Dixon, Tony Adams, David Platt, Patrick Vieira, Ian Wright, Dennis Bergkamp, Paul Merson and a young Nicolas Anelka, and their form was to get them a Champions League place.

Derby took the lead quite early in the game (six minutes) which started from a Derby goal-kick that came to Ashley Ward. A series of passes between Ward, both Powells and Trollope released Asanovic on the left. His high, hanging cross saw Ward out-jump two Arsenal defenders and head the ball down. With Seamen standing still, the ball hit the foot of the post and bounced up head high again and Ward was the first to react and was on hand to nod the ball into the empty net, and score what was to be Derby's last goal at the Normanton End of the ground. Paul Merson immediately hobbled off injured and was replaced by Nikolas Anelka.

Derby were undoubtedly the better team and, from their point of view, the game swung heavily in their favour when Tony Adams was sent off after just 11 minutes. On eight minutes he had flattened Asanovic and was given a yellow card. Three minutes later, Adams himself took a quick free-kick that was aimed for Ian Wright, but Daryll Powell intercepted it, and as he approached halfway he was recklessly tackled by Adams, which left the referee with little option but to dismiss the England defender.

After some re-organisation within the Arsenal defence, Derby spurned a couple of good chances to increase their lead. The best chance fell to Ward following a good piece of play from Gary Rowett to beat a defender and send over an inviting cross. Ward was marked by Lee Dixon who was no match for the attacker, particularly anything in the air, and his diving header went a couple of feet wide, again with the goalkeeper stranded not making any attempt to make a save.

Derby had the better of the first half and fully deserved their interval lead against a 10-man Arsenal team, and really should have had at least one more goal. The turning point in the game came with the substitution of Paul McGrath on 55 minutes to be replaced by midfielder Lee Carsley. This being McGrath's final appearance in League football it was marked with a standing ovation from both sets of fans after a long and successful career at Aston Villa, Manchester United and the Republic of Ireland. One feels that if that substitution had happened 10 minutes from the end of the game instead of 10 minutes into the second half, the scoreline would have been different.

McGrath later had a change of heart and appeared for Sheffield United for part of the following season.

The Arsenal equaliser came when Anelka was allowed to run a long way before being challenged and he managed to get a shot on target which Mart Poom could not hold and parried it into the path of Ian Wright. Wright used all his experience and skill and calmly lifted the ball over the goalkeeper from 8 yards.

Arsenal took the lead with a wonderful piece of skill from Dutchman Dennis Bergkamp. A speculative shot from Ray Parlour from 35 yards out was flicked on by Bergkamp towards the side of the area in space. As he ran on, Poom started to rush out to block any potential shot, but Bergkamp produced a wonderful chip that left the Derby goalkeeper stranded.

As the game approached the final whistle, Arsenal worked another piece of magic to produce another goal for Ian Wright, his 30th of the season. Bergkamp split the defence with a pass to the goal area where Wright managed to get the final touch despite the attention of two defenders and Poom.

Jim Smith was probably guilty of making substitutions too early, particularly that of McGrath who maybe could have played longer and still got the same appreciation from the crowd without upsetting the teams shape and balance and allowing the Arsenal forwards more room to play. Arsenal, though, when they set about the task of winning the football match were far superior and showed how much further Derby had to go before they could compete against the very top teams.

One telling statistic from the game was the attendance of 18,287, which was actually the highest of the season and was the highest since the stadium became all seated on all sides and underlines how critical to the club that the move to Pride Park was to become, where attendances of over 30,000 could be accommodated with ease and comfort for all supporters, with unobstructed views.

Derby's first season in the Premier League had come to a successful conclusion, with the main priority being to establish themselves in the division (which they did with some terrific home performances and that astonishing win at Old Trafford) and to ensure they retain their status and build on it in the following years, especially as they had the new stadium to move to during the summer.

Although this game was the last League game to be played at the Baseball Ground, Martin Taylor had his testimonial match the following week and it was still used for training (until the Moor Farm complex was completed), reserve and youth-team matches for several years to come.

Arsenal finished the season in third place on goal difference, just three goals behind Newcastle United, with Manchester United some seven points clear. Derby were comfortably in 12th position, level on points with Leeds United and Tottenham Hotspur. Relegated that year were Sunderland, Middlesbrough (who were deducted points for failing to fulfill a fixture at Blackburn due to an extensive injury list) and Nottingham Forest.

ASHLEY WARD

Born: 24 November 1970

Debut v Norwich City (away), Division One, 23 March 1996 lost 0–1

Last game v Barnsley (home), Premier League, 30 August 1997, won 1–0

First goal v West Bromwich Albion (away), Division One, 5 May 1996, lost 2–3

Bought from: Norwich City

Sold to: Barnsley

Total appearances: 35 + 9 subs, 12 goals

Consecutive games: 19, from 14 September 1996 to 18 January 1997

Ashley Ward was one of those players who moved from club to club every couple of years (Manchester City, Leicester City, Crewe Alexandra and Norwich City) before

joining Derby during the 1995–96 season from Norwich City for £1 million. He was signed to provide additional striking power in the push for promotion, but he struggled with injury in his first few months, eventually scoring in the last match of the season.

Ward had the honour of scoring the last Derby goal scored at the Baseball Ground and would have been the first scorer at Pride Park but for a floodlight failure that caused the game against Wimbledon to be abandoned. A few weeks later he was sold to Barnsley for £1.3 million in September 1997.

In an unusual twist his first game after signing from Norwich City was against Norwich and he was sold to the team he played in his last game, Barnsley.

DERBY COUNTY 0
SAMPDORIA 1

Pre-Season Friendly   **Wednesday 4 August 1997**

Pride Park Stadium

Derby County: Poom, Laursen (Flynn, 87), Stimac (Yates, 87), Dailly, Eranio (Rowett, 77), van der Laan (Trollope, 77), D. Powell (Carsley, 45), Asanovic (Hunt, 45), C. Powell, Ward (Carbon, 62), Baiano (Simpson, 67). Other sub: Hoult.

Sampdoria: Ferron, Balleri, Mannini, Pesaresi, Laigle, Mihajlovic, Matute (Scarchilli, 62), Veron (Francescetti, 80), Boghossian, Klinsmann (Tovalieri, 67), Montella (Salsano, 82). Other subs: Ambrosio, Hugo, Vergassola, Dichio, Dieng.

Referee: D.J. Gallagher (Banbury)

Attendance: 29,041

After 18 months since the announcement was made, Derby County finally moved into their new home, now officially called Pride Park Stadium, during the summer months of 1997, in readiness for the start of the 1997–98 season.

Driven by local property developer Peter Gadsby and with backing from chairman Lionel Pickering, the stadium had been designed by The Miller Partnership and was based on Middlesbrough's new stadium built a couple of years previously. There were over 30 actual differences in design between the two stadiums, Derby learning from the feedback from the North East. The publicity material issued by Derby used photos of the interior – these were actually of the Middlesbrough stadium with the seats coloured black instead of red.

The Queen was formerly invited to open the stadium the previous week (18 July) in front a capacity crowd of school parties, local groups, fans, invited guests from the world of football, former players and a host of celebrities and politicians who were known to be fans of the club. The gala celebrations started early in the

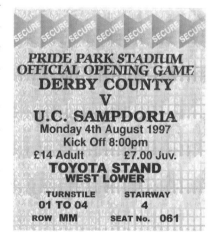

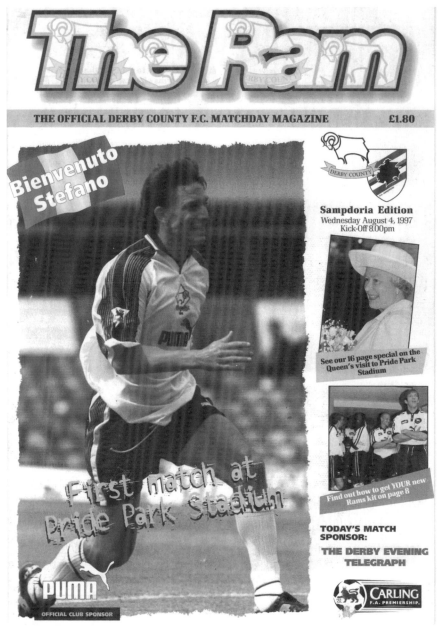

day before the Queen arrived when she formerly unveiled a commemorative stone and was introduced to the Derby players by the owner, Lionel Pickering, and manager Jim Smith.

To mark the first game at the new stadium, Derby had managed to secure a friendly against one of the top Italian teams of the time, Sampdoria, although many fans would have preferred to play a foreign team where Derby had played in their European Cup

The Opening of Pride Park Stadium

by Her Majesty The Queen
Friday, July 18th 1997

This publication kindly sponsored by

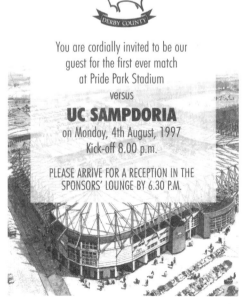

You are cordially invited to be our
guest for the first ever match
at Pride Park Stadium

versus

UC SAMPDORIA

on Monday, 4th August, 1997
Kick-off 8.00 p.m.

PLEASE ARRIVE FOR A RECEPTION IN THE
SPONSORS' LOUNGE BY 6.30 P.M.

days, Benfica or Juventus, although their own pre-season arrangements may have made that impossible.

Prior to the game a host of former players, nearly 50 from various eras, were greeted onto the field and presented with a replica shirt with their name on the back. Kevin Hector received probably the biggest cheer of the night, as he is rarely seen as part of public events, preferring to keep himself to himself.

Derby's second season in the Premier League saw some additions to the playing squad – Italians Stefano Eranio (from AC Milan and who would have been part of Italy's World Cup squad in 1994, until a broken leg forced him out of the squad) and Francesco Baiano (a small, skilful striker from Fiorentina) had arrived, as had Jonathan Hunt from Birmingham City. Players who had left during the close season and missed out on the opportunity of playing at Pride Park were Paul McGrath (Sheffield United), Martin Taylor (Wycombe Wanderers), Marco Gabbiadini (unattached) and Darren Wassall (Birmingham City).

The Italian team's star players of Mihajlovic, Veron and Klinsmann (the German national captain and a summer signing) all started the game and among the substitutes was Danny Dichio (another new signing from Queen's Park Rangers), who was later to play for Derby when on loan during the 2003–04 season. Their coach, who had been newly appointed, was Cesar Luis Menotti who had previously managed Barcelona and won the World Cup in 1978 with Argentina.

Derby's options, particularly up front, were limited by injury – both Sturridge and Wanchope had undergone knee operations and were several weeks away from playing again and Willems had taken a knock on his ankle during a pre-season game at Oxford United. Igor Stimac was a welcome name on the teamsheet, hoping that his spell of injuries was now behind him (he was only able to play half of the previous season) and able to marshall the defence, which lined up with three central defenders in Stimac, Dailly and Laursen, with Eranio and Powell as the wing-backs.

Being a pre-season match, it was never going to be a classic game of thunderous tackles and non-stop attacking, and was always likely to become a scrappy affair once the inevitable second-half substitutions started. The lure of the new stadium and its facilities and one of Europe's top teams of the time meant that over 29,000 fans attended the game – Derby's highest home attendance since February 1983 when Manchester United visited the Baseball Ground for an FA Cup tie.

After all the anticipation and formalities, the first game at the new stadium could finally get under way. Derby started brightly in their new surroundings, and the new striker immediately caught the eye, not only because he was small, but he looked to have an eye for goal which is a precious commodity and necessary in the Premier League. On 37 minutes he had a header that just went the wrong side of the post from a cross by Chris Powell, and shortly afterwards he forced the Italian 'keeper Fabrizio Ferron to dive at his feet as he was about to shoot.

As the game settled down, Sampdoria got into their stride in only their second pre-season game and became more dangerous, with Jurgen Klinsmann wanting to impress his new employers and fans that had made the trip from Genoa. Mart Poom was getting plenty of practice at shot stopping – Klinsmann, Montella and a Mihajlovic free-kick all were dealt with competently.

As the second half got under way, the substitutions started, with Lee Carsley and Jonathan Hunt coming on to replace Daryll Powell and Asanovic. It was Hunt who set up Stimac to have a shot on target that had the goalkeeper scrambling around. Ashley Ward nearly gave Derby a 54th-minute lead, but 'keeper Ferron came racing off his line and blocked the goal attempt.

Vincenzo Montella's goal just before the hour was worth waiting for and suitable for the opening of any stadium and showed a glimpse of how he scored 24 goals in 34 games and had been brought into the Italian national squad. A through ball left Christian Dailly running alongside Montella and trying to force him away from the goal area. Neither Dailly nor Poom were expecting him to shoot from such a position, and the swerve and power in the shot left Poom unable to reach it.

Stimac had another opportunity shortly afterwards but his header from Stefano Eranio's cross was not good enough to beat the 'keeper. Montella had a good opportunity to extend the lead when Sandro Tovalieri played him through, but Mart Poom came to Derby's rescue.

The main star of the Italian side on the night was the Argentinian player Juan Sebastian Veron, whom Maradonna said was the 'best midfielder in the world', and he eventually played in the English Premier League, firstly with Manchester United and then Chelsea.

As usual for these pre-season games, there was a large number of substitutions made during the second half, which more often than not, destroys any pattern or flow to the game and does not give the players time to settle into the game. Derby made eight changes with only Poom, Dailly and Chris Powell playing for the full 90 minutes and the new player Eranio, Baiano and Hunt all playing at least half the game in front of the home fans for the first time.

Managers will always say that the results in pre-season do not matter, but it is the players' fitness that is important and style of play. For this game, it was probably more about the occasion and getting the players, new and old, used to playing in front of large crowds again and, more importantly, in the new surroundings they would be calling home from now onwards.

Derby had asked the League for the first couple of games to be away games so that any last-minute finishing touches around the stadium, both internally and externally, could be finished off. The first home League game was a mid-week encounter with Wimbledon. Derby were winning the game 2–1 thanks to an Ashley Ward goal (making him the last scorer at the Baseball Ground and first at Pride Park), however a floodlight failure after 11 minutes of the second half of the game meant that the game was abandoned. There were some strong rumours at the time that the floodlight failure was somehow part of a Far East betting scandal, but the club was cleared of any involvement and no evidence was ever found to support it.

The honour of the first Pride Park goal went to Stefano Eranio, who scored a penalty in 1–0 win over Barnsley at the end of August.

MART POOM

Born: 3 February 1972

Debut v Manchester United (away), Premier League, 5 April 1997, won 3–2

Last game v Sheffield Wednesday (away), Division One, 2 November 2002, won 3–1

Bought from: SC Flora Tallinn, Estonia

Sold to: Sunderland

Total appearances: 162 + 3 subs

Consecutive games: 56 from 20 November 1999 to 30 January 2001

Mart Poom had already been signed by Jim Smith once when he was manager of Portsmouth, so it was no real surprise, when Russell Hoult's form wavered, that Smith paid £500,000 to bring him back to England. He made his debut at Old Trafford in the same game as Paulo Wanchope and it took him a while to establish himself as first choice.

At 6ft 4in, he was able to dominate his penalty area but was also a good shot stopper and very agile. He was a hugely popular figure with the fans with a chorus of 'Pooooom' whenever he touched the ball and he was voted as Player of the Year for the 1999–2000 season. He was the Estonian international goalkeeper and went on to make 120 appearances for the national side.

Poom moved to Sunderland for £2.5 million in November 2002 and returned in September 2003 and famously scored a last-minute equaliser at Pride Park with a towering header.

SHEFFIELD WEDNESDAY 2
DERBY COUNTY 5

Premier League   **24 September 1997**

Hillsborough

Sheffield Wednesday: Clarke, Blondeau, Newsome (Nicol, 27), Walker, Nolan, Whittingham (Collins, 61), Magilton, Clough (Hirst, 45), Pembridge, Carbone, Di Canio. Other subs: Briscoe, Grobbelaar (gk).

Derby County: Poom, Dailly, Stimac, Laursen, Rowett, Eranio, Carsley, C. Powell, Baiano (Hunt, 81), Wanchope, Burton. Other subs: Hoult (gk), van der Laan, Simpson, Trollope.

Referee: M.D. Reed (Birmingham)

Attendance: 22,391

Both teams came into this mid-week game after an indifferent start to the Premier League season, Wednesday sitting one point and one place off the bottom and Derby sitting in 14th place just one point better off. Wednesday's results had included a 7–2 defeat at Blackburn Rovers and a 2–0 defeat at Grimsby Town in the opening round of the League Cup, and manager David Pleat was starting to come under pressure to get some more positive results.

Derby's form was, at best, average – winning two and losing three of their first five League games in their second Premier League season, scoring and conceding five goals, but their recent form was good, winning three out of the last four games. On paper, both squads were full of attacking talent with a wealth of foreign talent available for selection; Wednesday having the likes of Des Walker, Benito Carbone, Paulo Di Canio, Steve Nicol, Bruce Grobelaar, Nigel Clough and Paul Hirst up against Igor Stimac, Jacob Laursen, Stefano Eranio, Paulo Wanchope, Francesco Baiano and Aljosa Asanovic for Derby.

Wednesday had to give a full debut to former

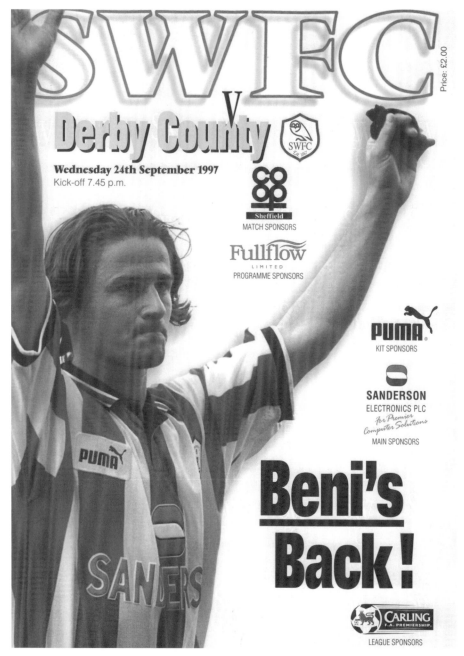

Rotherham goalkeeper Clarke as Kevin Pressman had suffered an injury during the weekend's fixture. Up front, Carbone returned following a three-match suspension following his sending off against Blackburn in that heavy defeat.

Going into the game, there was the usual statistic banded about by the media saying that Derby had not won at Hillsborough since a 3–2 win in September 1936, and this also included three FA Cup semi-finals (even the 1946 Cup-winning team could not win there, being taken to a replay by Birmingham City).

Jim Smith made three changes to the starting line-up following the weekend 2–1 defeat at Aston Villa – Stimac, Burton and Wanchope coming in for Trollope, Hunt and the injured Dean Sturridge. Baiano would have been keen to get on the scoresheet, having broken his duck in English football with his goal at the weekend.

The 22,391 fans that turned up for this fixture were treated to a marvellous game that had a bit of everything (seven goals, a penalty and a sending off) and three goals in the first 12 minutes. Not everything went Derby's way, with the defence looking likely to concede a goal at any time in the first half but, having got their noses in front by half-time, there was only going to be one winner.

Paulo Di Canio scored the first goal for the home team after just four minutes when he latched onto a pass from Carbone, following an excellent interchange with Pembridge, and he curled a shot across Poom from an acute angle. The joy of the home fans lasted barely three minutes as Derby produced a magnificent move involving five players as Dailly's pass was directed onto Gary Rowett by Wanchope. Rowett, who was playing in his normal role of the attacking right-back following the return of Stimac to the team, saw his cross expertly nodded down by Deon Burton and the little Italian, Baiano, steered his half-volley shot past Clarke in the Wednesday goal from the edge of the penalty area.

Within five minutes, Rowett was the culprit as he clipped Di Canio's heels inside the box. Carbone took the kick (but only just scored, as Poom dived the right way) to score his fifth goal of the season. With the game still wide open, an Eranio corner in the 27th minute found Wanchope, whose shot was initially blocked and not cleared by the defence, and came out to Jacob Laursen. His shot flew through a crowded area and nestled in the back of the net, 2–2. Wednesday's rock of a defender, Jon Newsome, was forced off through injury and consequently the home team's defence fell apart and every Derby attack could have ended in another goal.

Derby took the lead for the first time on 32 minutes with a Wanchope header after a left-wing cross. This time it came from Chris Powell, which was nodded on, once again, by Burton. This was the Costa Rican's first goal since he burst onto the Premiership scene with that jaw-dropping goal at Old Trafford in April. A further Wanchope header was also cleared off the line in the first half.

Wednesday had to make changes, and Nigel Clough was replaced by David Hirst at the break with the intention of getting a goal to get them back level. Their plans were quickly in ruins as Derby poured forward two minutes into the second half, with Eranio crossing for Baiano to skilfully score his second of the night, controlling the cross with his left foot before shooting with his right past a defence and goalkeeper that were just spectators.

Baiano should have completed his hat-trick a minute later with a free header from 10 yards that shaved the left-hand post, and Wanchope was left one-on-one with the 'keeper on a through ball from Baiano, but for once Clarke got his hands to the ball and saved well.

The game had been won by Derby long ago, but it became a case of when they would take their foot off the pedal before Blondeau was sent off after bringing down Burton on 68 minutes, this being the Frenchman's first game since August. Having used all their substitutes, Wednesday were in dis-array, further compounded when Burton scored his first goal for Derby after a superb piece of skill from Wanchope on the left wing.

The home crowd drifted away in disgust as they saw their team slump to a new low, with chants of 'Pleat Out, Pleat Out'. Carbone had an altercation with his teammate David Hirst and just walked off the field – eventually returning after some persuasion from the Wednesday bench.

As Gerald Mortimer said in the opening comment of his match report in the *Derby Evening Telegraph*, 'Derby County's exuberant attacking was too much for Sheffield Wednesday and left manager David Pleat with a pile of trouble.'

Derby's first away win of the season was complete in an emphatic scoreline, that could easily have been more, and also an impressive attacking display that was repeated on the following Saturday in a 4–0 rout of Southampton. The success was built on an energetic midfield of Eranio and Carsley, with Burton and the unpredictable Wanchope as the strikers and Baiano playing just behind them.

Derby's win lifted them into 12th place, just three points outside the top six teams after the first six games of the season. David Pleat's position as Wednesday manager lasted for a further five weeks before he was sacked.

FRANCESCO BAIANO

Born: 24 February 1968
Debut v Barnsley (home), Premier League, 30 August 1997, won 1–0
Last game v Newcastle United (away), Premier League, 25 October 1999, lost 0–2
First goal v Aston Villa (away), Premier League, 20 September 1997, lost 1–2
Bought from: Fiorentina, Italy
Sold to: Ternana, Italy
Total appearances: 63 + 12 subs, 19 goals

Consecutive appearances: 23 from 30 August 1997 to 7 February 1998

The diminutive striker, standing only 5ft 7in, arrived in Derby a few weeks after Stefano Eranio who had recommended him to Jim Smith. He had played for six Italian clubs, scoring regularly wherever he played and had also been capped by Italy on two occasions in 1991. Nicknamed 'Cicco', unlike many of Derby's other foreign imports of that era he never tried to learn the English language and relied on Eranio to act as interpreter.

He cost Derby £1.5 million from Fiorentina, where he had a famous partnership with the Argentine striker Gabriel Batistuta where they were known as the 'Ba-Ba' strikers. He was technically excellent, with an eye for goal and filled the hole behind the main forwards of Sturridge and Wanchope, making that particular forward line one of the most varied and deadly on its day. This combination was probably the most attacking forward line seen at Pride Park.

In his first season he equalled a club record by scoring in six consecutive games from 20 September 1997 through to 22 October 1997.

LEEDS UNITED 4
DERBY COUNTY 3

Premier League   **Saturday 8 November 1997**

Elland Road

Leeds United: Martyn, Maybury (Bowyer, 45), Wetherall, Radebe, Robertson, Kelly, Haaland, Hopkin (Hasselbaink, 76), Ribeiro, Wallace, Kewell. Other subs: Beeney (gk), Harte, Holenaar.

Derby County: Poom, Laursen, Dailly, Carbon (Kozluk, 53), Rowett, Carsley, D. Powell (Hunt, 84), C. Powell, Sturridge, Baiano, Asanovic (Trollope, 82). Other subs: Hoult (gk), Willems.

Referee: N.S. Barry (Scunthorpe)

Attendance: 33,572

Derby County and Leeds United met at Elland Road when they were level in the League table on 20 points, Derby having played 12 games, one fewer than their hosts, and lying in a respectable seventh place.

Leeds's current form was good, with one defeat in the previous six games, which included wins against Manchester United, Newcastle United and Tottenham Hotspur.

Paulo Wanchope had won the October Player of the Month award, based on the SKY/Opta Index, but like his Costa Rican compatriot Mauricio Solis he was unavailable for this match as they had an important World Cup qualifying match to play against Mexico.

In his programme notes, the Leeds manager George Graham said of Wanchope's enforced absence, 'it is good for our defenders but it's a sad day for the fans'. Since his debut against Manchester United in April, Wanchope had now become a house hold name and had now settled into English football and had scored twice the previous weekend in a 3–0 against Arsenal at Pride Park.

Leeds were able to name an unchanged team from the one that won 1–0 at Tottenham Hotspur the previous weekend, meaning there was no place in the starting line-up for Jimmy Floyd Hasselbaink and Lee Bowyer.

Derby's record had not been great at Elland Road, their last win being during the 1974–75 Championship season when a last-minute Francis Lee goal gave Derby a 1–0

win. The current team were in need of some points away from Pride Park, having lost four of their opening six away League games, and the away form would be a major impact on their potential League position.

Derby got off to a perfect start with just four minutes gone thanks largely to an horrendous goalkeeping error from the Leeds goalkeeper Nigel Martyn. The move started with a superb cross-field ball from Gary Rowett to Asanovic, who controlled the ball superbly before laying it out to Chris Powell, who had made an overlap run down the edge of the penalty area. His overhit cross was headed back towards his own goal by David Robertson. Martyn, unchallenged, should have tipped it over the bar for a corner but instead caught it and then realised his momentum would have carried him into the back of the net. His only alternative was to drop the ball and Sturridge was at his feet to tap the ball over the line.

A routine save by Poom on 10 minutes at one end started the move for a second goal a few seconds later, again Martyn being at fault. Poom's long clearance caught the Leeds defence back peddling and, as the ball bounced, Sturridge outpaced Radebe and, as Martyn rushed out to the edge of the penalty area, simply lifted it past him and into an empty net for his fifth goal of the season.

Derby were two goals to the good, without having to work very hard for them.

Sturridge was having one of those days where everything he did worked, or he was in the right place at the right time. The third goal just after the half-hour mark was a result of his pace – starting in his own half and aided by a return pass from Baiano. His pace took him clear down the right wing and away from the defenders.

As he was about to shoot he was brought down by Robertson, who was booked by referee Neil Barry for the deliberate foul. Asanovic was the assigned penalty taker, Sturridge resisting the temptation to go for his hat-trick. His spot-kick sent the goalkeeper the wrong way as he hit it high to his left.

Although the 3–0 scoreline was slightly flattering, it was by no means one way traffic, with Kelly's corners always causing concern among the Derby defence and Poom having to make several smart saves.

What Derby needed now was an experienced central defender, not easily ruffled, to see out the last 15 minutes of the first half without incident. Stimac would have fitted the bill perfectly, but he was ruled out through injury until the new year. Instead, Derby had the young and inexperienced Matt Carbon and Gary Rowett. In the 10 minutes before half-time Leeds scored two goals – the first, on 37 minutes, a little lucky as a long-range shot from Bruno Ribero flicked off Rod Wallace's foot and past Poom, who had the original shot covered. This was the turning point in the game as the Derby defence collapsed.

As half-time approached, Leeds scored again when Darryl Powell could only half-clear a corner and it fell nicely for the Australian Harry Kewell, who hit a superb volley through a crowd of players around the goal area and past the Derby 'keeper. There was even time for Chris Powell to clear a chance off the line from Alf-Inge Haaland as Leeds began to sense that the game was very much alive.

A half-time substitution by Leeds saw full-back Maybury replaced by Lee Bowyer as their intentions were clear. The half-time break and talk by Jim Smith and Steve McClaren did little to stop the continuing panic in the Derby defence throughout the second half, as several good chances to equalise came and went for the Yorkshire team.

Part of the problem was that the defenders were panicking and instead of trying to play football from defence through midfield, they began clearing the ball anywhere they could and without the height of Wanchope up front, the two Derby forwards of Baiano and Sturridge were not tall enough to keep the ball and it kept heading straight back towards the Derby goal.

Matt Carbon left the field early in the second half being replaced by Rob Kozluk. It was not until the 76th minute that Hasselbaink was introduced, replacing midfielder Hopkin, trying to take advantage of the inexperienced defence. For all the chances Leeds were having, it was not until the 81st minute that they grabbed an equaliser – a soft goal from Derby's point of view as Christian Dailly handled the ball from yet another corner kick. Hasselbaink, who had only been on the field for five minutes, calmly rolled the ball into Poom's bottom-left-hand corner. Poom was unable to read the penalty and never moved.

Immediately, Derby took off Asanovic and replaced him with Paul Trollope, a more defensive move, indicating that Derby would be happy to play out the remaining few minutes and escape with a draw. Despite the defensive change, in the 90th minute, the inevitable fourth and winning Leeds goal came and sent the home fans wild with delight. Hasselbaink beat Dailly and pulled in a low cross that Bowyer met with a thumping shot in front of the home fans.

Had Derby won, they would have climbed to fourth place in the Premier League. Derby coach Steve McClaren said afterwards that the defeat was a 'major blow to confidence and self belief'.

Despite the fact that it was an exciting game for the neutral fans, and indeed, both sets of fans would have experienced all sorts of emotions during the game, it was a worrying defensive performance once the first Leeds goal went in. This game turned out to be Aljosa Asanovic's last for Derby.

ALJOSA ASANOVIC

Born: 14 December 1965
Debut v Leeds United (home), Premier League, 17 August 1996, draw 3–3
Last game v Leeds United (away), Premier League, 8 November 1997, lost 3–4

First goal v Sunderland (home), Premier League, 14 September 1996, won 1–0

Bought from: Hadjuk Split, Croatia

Sold to: Napoli, Italy

Total appearance: 42 + 1 subs, 7 goals

Consecutive games: 12 from 25 January 1997 to 22 March 1997

Aljosa Asanovic joined Derby in the weeks before the Euro '96 tournament to join his Croation teammate Igor Stimac. It would be fair to say that few Derby fans would have heard of him before that point in time.

He was nicknamed 'Vatreni Lakat' (meaning 'fiery elbow') in Croatia for his style of running with his elbows pointed out, moving opposing players out of the way. He is one of the many talented footballers of the 1990s to be of gypsy (Romany) origin. He was a tall, left-sided midfield player and had played for six clubs before joining Derby and a further five afterwards, having a reputation for staying a year or two at each club before moving on. He was the first player to score for the newly formed country of Croatia in a game against USA in October 1990.

DERBY COUNTY 1
BARCELONA 3

Pre-season friendly   Friday 7 August 1998

Pride Park Stadium

Derby County: Poom, Delap (Kozluk, 76), Schnoor, Carsley, Dailly (Burton, 80), Laursen, Eranio (Rowett, 37), Sturridge, Wanchope, Bohinen (Hunt, 86), Powell. Other subs: Hoult, Elliott, Carbonari, Bridge-Wilkinson.

Barcelona: Baia, Okunowo (Reiziger, 60), Nadal, Abelardo, Roger Garcia, Xavi (Cocu, 60), Figo, Ciric (Anderson, 45), Luis Enrique (Giovanni, 60), Oscar Garcia (Rivaldo, 60), Jofre (Zenden, 60). Other subs: Ferron, Arnau, Oscar Alvarez, Mario, Babangida.

Referee: D.J. Gallagher (Banbury).

Attendance: 29,739.

The quality of pre-season friendly opposition had reached new heights with the 1998–99 season home pre-season friendly match which brought Barcelona to Pride Park Stadium. Spain, as usual at that time, had been a major disappointment in the France '98 World Cup tournament, failing to get past the first-round group stage, despite winning their last game 6–1.

Christian Dailly returned from a personally successful World Cup tournament, playing in all three of Scotland's matches in Group A, but he could not help them avoid finishing bottom of that particular qualification group. Derby had four other representatives at the tournament – Deon Burton and Daryll Powell (both Jamaica), Jacob Laursen (Denmark) and Igor Stimac (for third-placed Croatia).

Summer moves had seen former captain Robbie van der Laan move to Barnsley and former Player of the Years Chris Powell and Dean Yates moving to Charlton Athletic and Watford respectively.

Mauricio Solis, signed at the same time as Wanchope, had returned to Costa Rica as his first team chances were limited due to non-EC player rules and his work permit was not renewed. Ron Willems and Jonathan Hunt were both deemed surplus and would be allowed to leave. Coming in were Argentinian defender Horacio Carbonari, Derby's record signing for £2.7 million from Club Rosario Central and left-back Stefan Schnoor from SV Hamburg, Germany on a free transfer.

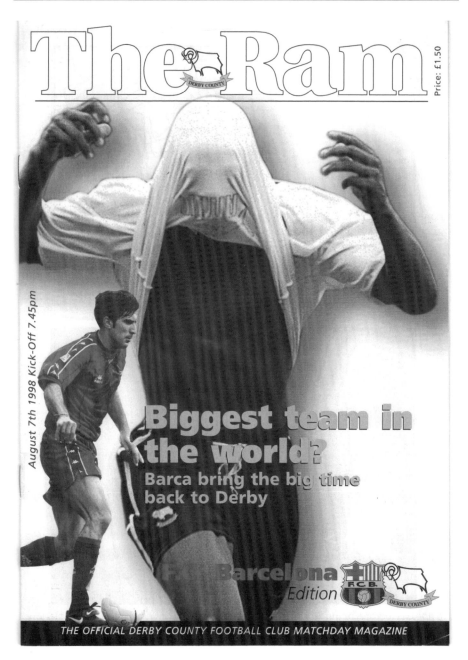

Derby's pre-season results were not great – defeats to Huddersfield Town, Scunthorpe United and Carlisle United were followed by a win at Bradford City and a Derbyshire Centenary Cup win over Chesterfield (on penalties). Francesco Baiano had picked up a calf injury during one of the games and was under constant treatment to get him fit for the start of the season and was not going to be risked.

Barcelona could boast to be one of the biggest club sides in the world and have a stadium to match, the 120,000 all-seater Camp Nou Stadium. Full of World Cup stars, they had also had some famous managers – Johan Cruyff, Terry Venables, Bobby Robson and were now coached by Dutchman Louis Van Gaal. Their starting line-up excluded many of the stars, but they were initially named among the substitutes so the Derby fans were hopeful of seeing them at some point during the game.

It was a warm evening, as expected for early August, and a large crowd had turned out to see the Barcelona stars play Derby for the first time and also possibly get a look at the new record signing Carbonari. Dean Sturridge saw plenty of the ball early on and had one or two runs and crosses that were easily dealt with by the visiting defence.

Luis Figo, the Portuguese playmaker and Barcelona captain, was instrumental in everything Barcelona did, and his corner on 15 minutes brought the first goal. His corner ballooned off Rory Delap's head, and Spanish striker Louis Enrique pounced at the back post and scored with a smartly hit volley from eight yards into the net.

Five minutes later the Spanish team were 2–0 up. Dragan Ciric beat Stefan Schnoor on the left wing and fired over a cross, and the ball fell to Figo to shoot at goal. Mart Poom could only parry the shot and present Oscar Garcia with the easiest of chances.

It was only now that the Derby players seemed to wake up and play their own football instead of watching Barcelona play theirs. Within a minute, Wanchope showed a flash of what he is capable of when he controlled the ball and lobbed the ball over the Barcelona goalkeeper, Vitor Baia, but his shot bounced off the bar.

A minute later he would get his name on the scoresheet. Rory Delap spotted Eranio's intelligent run to the edge of the penalty area and the Italian moved the ball forward to Bohinen who was unable to turn and shoot himself so he passed to Wanchope who side-footed home from six yards out. Derby were now in control of the game and pressing for an equaliser. Dean Sturridge was causing problems with his pace and on 24 minutes found himself with just the 'keeper to beat, but the ball ran away from him.

After 37 minutes Derby suffered a major injury scare when Eranio went through two hard tackles before being hit by a third, hard from behind by the goalscorer Oscar Garcia. The *Sporting Life* described the incident as '[Eranio] had to endure a barrage of venomous Barca tackles'. Gary Rowett had to replace him. The resulting Laursen free-kick went through the defensive wall but was straight at the 'keeper.

Fernandez Abelardo helped out his goalkeeper when Wanchope flicked the ball past the rushing Baia and, being new to the Premiership and not yet fully exposed to the wider European audience, Wanchope's unpredictability and awkwardness was causing problems for the Spanish defence who were not sure how best to handle him. The famous, or infamous, 'Beast of Barcelona', Miguel Nadal, could not get near him at times towards the end of the first half. Eventually Nadal got tired of watching Wanchope go past him and body checked him at the next opportunity.

Derby continued to create chances after the half-time interval – a Bohinen shot was deflected over; Wanchope shot wide following one of his mazy runs; and Sturridge was denied by the 'keeper after a through ball from Dailly.

On the hour, the Barcelona coach brought on the World Cup stars in one go – Dutchmen Michael Reiziger, Philip Cocu and Boudewiin Zenden and Brazilians Rivaldo and Giovanni – and from that point onwards they took control of the game and soon put it beyond Derby. Zenden's pace on the left was the catalyst, and from one of his runs and crosses on 76 minutes, as Anderson failed to make contact, the ball went in off Laursen's boot to leave Poom stranded.

There were two opportunities to narrow the scoreline late in the game. First a Wanchope shot trickled past the post and then Deon Burton, a substitute for Dailly, missed a shot in front of goal.

It was hard to draw any conclusions from this result as neither team was at full strength and although Derby had control of the middle part of the game they did not create many clear chances and as soon as Barcelona made their substitutions the game quickly went away from Derby. Carbonari did not feature in the game, which seems strange.

Derby finished their pre-season with just two wins from their six games, one on penalties and the other in a testimonial game. This game was to be the last appearance at Pride Park for Gary Rowett and Christian Dailly. Birmingham City made a good offer for Rowett and Blackburn Rovers (who Dailly played against in the opening game in the first Premier League game of the season on 15 August) made an unbelievable offer of £5.35 million for his services. This depleted Derby's defence of two experienced players during the first week of the season.

STEFANO ERANIO

Born: 29 December 1966
Debut v Blackburn Rovers (away), Premier League, 9 August 1997, lost 0–1
Last game v Ipswich Town (home), Premier League, 19 May 2001, draw 1–1
First goal v Barnsley (home), Premier League, 30 August 1997, won 1–0
Bought from: AC Milan, Italy
Sold to: Released

Total appearances: 96 + 12 subs, 10 goals
Consecutive games: 12 from 24 April 1999 to 11 September 1999

Stefano Eranio was an Italian international player and had won many domestic trophies and played in two Champions League Finals with his club, AC Milan. He joined Derby in time for the opening of Pride Park and scored the first goal at the stadium in a competitive game. He suffered a broken leg in November 1999 following a bad tackle at Liverpool and planned to retire at the end of the 2000–01 season, when he was given an emotional send-off. During the summer he was persuaded to come back but did not play again as Jim Smith was sacked and Eranio left. He was a gifted right-sided midfield player or full-back and fully deserved his place in the All-Time team and made a guest appearance in the Ted McMinn benefit game in 2006, where he was the best player on the field.

LIVERPOOL 1
DERBY COUNTY 2

Premier League   **Saturday 7 November 1998**

Anfield

Liverpool: James, Staunton, McManaman, Fowler, Owen, Redknapp, Heggem (Thompson 67), Berger (McAteer 32), Ince, Bjornebye, Carragher. Subs: Friedel, Kvarme, McAteer, Harkness, Thompson.
Derby County: Hoult, Carbonari, Powell, Dorigo, Wanchope, Delap (Kozluk, 73), Harper (Bridge-Wilkinson), Bohinen, Laursen, Elliot, Burton. Subs: Launders, Christie, Bridge-Wilkinson, Poom, Kozluk.
Referee: U. Rennie (Sheffield).
Attendance: 44,020

Liverpool had returned home from a midweek UEFA Cup tie against Valencia in buoyant mood and were now England's remaining representative in the competition. From 1–0 down with nine minutes to go they forced a 2–2 draw to go through on the away goals rule. It was tarnished, however, by the sendings off of Ince and McManaman at the end of the game.

Steve Elliott, who had recently had his 20th birthday, was not born when Derby last won at Anfield which was way back in February 1970 and Derby had suffered 10 consecutive defeats since then and only scored once during that time. Derby were not in good form, without a win in the last six games and they were crippled by a string of injuries to Francesco Baiano, Lee Carsley, Stefano Eranio, Spencer Prior, Igor Stimac and Dean Sturridge and Stefan Schnoor was suspended.

Resources were severely stretched, with three of the substitutes still to make their debuts – Marc Bridge-Wilkinson, Malcolm Christie and Brian Launders. Malcolm Christie had been signed from non-League Nuneaton Borough just two weeks ago and had barely played in the reserve team and now found himself at Anfield. Brian Launders had arrived on loan from Veendam and Bridge-Wilkinson was a former Derby youth player and reserve regular. More through circumstances than any tactical insight and planning, Derby went into the game with three forwards (Burton, Harper and Wanchope) and four midfielders, with Powell and Bohinen filling the central positions.

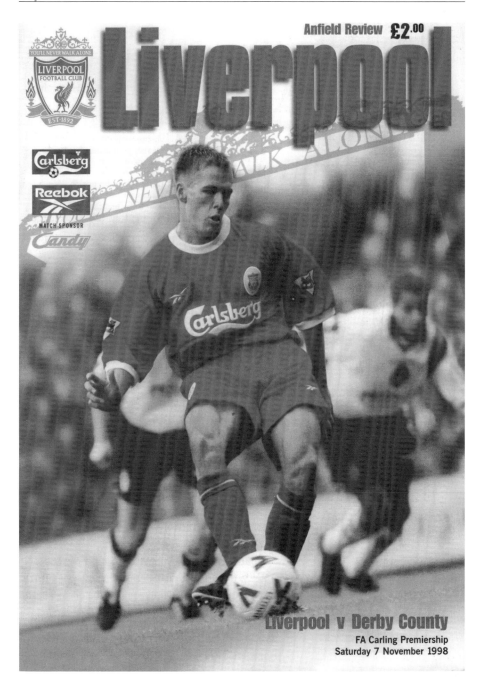

Anfield Review £2.⁰⁰

Liverpool v Derby County
FA Carling Premiership
Saturday 7 November 1998

Derby were attacking the Kop in the first half and it was something of a surprise, given the circumstances, when Derby took the lead after six minutes through Kevin Harper. Harper was making his first full start after previously making five substitute appearances since his £300,000 summer move from Hibs. The move started with Deon

Burton who passed to Tony Dorigo out on the left, and his cross was perfect and picked out Harper completely unmarked beyond the far post and looped his header back across David James into the net in front of the Kop.

Liverpool, as expected, were stung into action, and with 84 minutes to play they would still be confident of getting a positive result. Firstly, Redknapp played in Robbie Fowler, who lifted his shot over Russell Hoult but not with enough pace to reach the goal, and Steve Elliot was on hand to hack the ball clear. Michael Owen, who scored four goals in Liverpool's last home League game, saw his hard cross blocked by Elliot and out for a corner.

The closest they were to come in this spell of pressure came after 18 minutes, when Redknapp crossed another ball into the Derby area and was met by Robbie Fowler who put his header against the foot of the post. Five minutes later Owen's pass set Fowler in on goal, but just as he was about to shoot Steve Elliot, not for the first time in the game, produced a superb saving tackle.

Despite the pressure, Derby's defenders were standing firm, and whenever the pressure was relieved with a Derby break the Liverpool defenders were very nervous of the unpredictable Wanchope and what he was capable of producing.

On 27 minutes their fears became true when Wanchope doubled Derby's lead following an excellent move that started deep in the Derby half with Ince losing control of the ball. The telling pass came from Bohinen who hit a wonderful pass from the centre circle down to Harper near the right corner flag. He held the ball up and with Burton, Wanchope and Daryll Powell arriving in support played the ball back to Delap to cross the ball into the six-yard area where Wanchope rose above Vegard Heggem and his header gave James no chance, to score his first goal in seven games.

After 32 minutes Berger was replaced by Jason McAteer as Liverpool, despite having most of the play but now two goals down, needed to be more direct in their play as the Anfield crowd began to get more anxious.

Half-time allowed the Derby defence to have a breather and the management to keep minds focused on the task at hand and they were going to sit back and let Liverpool have the possession and try and catch them on the break as the Liverpool attacks would get increasingly frantic as the game went on. Jacob Laursen, Derby's captain on the day, was keeping calm and Horacio Carbonari was having a much better game than his previous ones since his multi-million pound summer move.

There were still chances for the Liverpool forwards as Fowler was left alone to run in from a Staunton corner but put his header wide and Owen managed to block a Hoult clearance, and despite the ball bouncing back over the goalkeeper's head there was no one nearby to take advantage.

On 67 minutes Liverpool made another substitution, taking off defender Heggem and replacing him with midfielder David Thompson in an attempt to overrun Derby's midfield and allow others to move further forward.

In response, Derby took off Delap and replaced him with a defender in Robert Kozluk. Liverpool finally broke through with just six minutes remaining when their best player on the day, Steve McManaman, got away from three Derby players and then knocked the ball and ran between Kozluk and Bohninen and squared the ball across the goal area for Jamie Redknapp to tap in. There were some late scares for Derby as the defenders became increasingly tired and this allowed McManaman to set up Redknapp again, but this time he fired over the bar.

Liverpool could not perform heroics for the second time in a week, and they slumped to their first League defeat at home since February and had won only one of the last eight League games.

Paul Walker (PA Sport) described the game as 'Liverpool's stars were ragged and shambolic at times as they failed to make any meaningful use of a vast amount of possession. And the front pairing of Robbie Fowler and Michael Owen rarely got the better of a stern, organised back-line'.

Liverpool's joint managership team of Gerard Houllier and Roy Evans was coming under increasing pressure as the duo struggled to make the partnership work. In fact, by the next League game, Roy Evans had resigned, leaving Houlier in sole charge.

Derby's players were naturally relieved, none more so than Carbonari who had struggled to settle since his move from South America, and this was the first time he was in a winning team. Steve Elliot, under the guidance of his more experienced defensive partners Carbonari and Laursen, was magnificent as the result moved Derby up to fifth place in the table, leapfrogging Liverpool.

Jim Smith commented that '...when suspensions and injuries hit big style as they did against Liverpool, you always hope players will come in and put pressure on senior professionals. They rarely do, but at Anfield Elliot, Harper and Carbonari came in and did well.'

Steve Elliot's performance during this game against international strikers Fowler and Owen saw him appear in the 'Team of Week' in five different national newspapers.

KEVIN HARPER

Born: 15 January 1976
Debut v Manchester City (home), League Cup, 16 September 1998, draw 1–1
Last game v Bolton Wanderers (home), League Cup, 13 October 1999, lost 1–2

First goal v Liverpool (away), Premier League, 7 November 1998, won 2–1

Bought from: Hibernian, Scotland

Sold to: Portsmouth

Total appearances: 7 + 34 subs, 2 goals

Consecutive games: 20 from 28 October 1998 to 20 February 1999

Kevin Harper was full of potential in his early career which earned him international honours for Scotland at B and Under-21 level as a small, pacey winger. It was this potential that persuaded Jim Smith to pay £300,000 for him on 10 September 1998 from Hibs.

He was primarily used as a substitute and rarely given a starting place. On one of these rare starts he helped Derby record only their seventh ever win at Liverpool with the opening goal. He was loaned out to Walsall in December 1999 and sold to Portsmouth the following March for £300,000, where he stayed for five years before moving to Stoke and then back to Scotland with Dunfermline.

NOTTINGHAM FOREST 2
DERBY COUNTY 2

Premier League   **Monday 16 November 1998**

City Ground

Nottingham Forest: Beasant, Rogers, Quashie, Chettle, Stone, Gemmill, Bart-Williams, Freedman (Harewood, 77), Armstrong, Bonalair, Van Hooijdonk. Other subs: Hjelde, Shipperley, Crossley, Gray.

Derby County: Hoult (Poom, 69), Carbonari, Powell, Dorigo, Wanchope, Prior, Harper (Sturridge, 40), Bohinen, Laursen, Elliot, Burton. Other subs: Baiano, Eranio, Bridge-Wilkinson.

Referee: G. Barber (Pyrford).

Attendance: 24,014.

Derby had won only one of their last six League games, and that was the previous weekend when they surprisingly won 2–1 at Liverpool which saw them climb to seventh place in the Premier League. This game had been moved to a Monday night for the benefit of live TV coverage.

For Forest, Pierre van Hooijdonk was playing his third game back following his self-imposed strike and time training on his own in his native Holland. All this came about as he wanted to be transferred, but the Forest owners refused. He received a lot of criticism from fans and teammates alike and watched from afar as Forest dropped to the bottom of the League, without a League win since the end of August (which was the third game of the season).

Derby's team was still suffering from injuries, Rory Delap was away in Yugoslavia with the Republic of Ireland squad, Rob Kozluk picked up an injury and Stefano Eranio was not match fit after his month out through injury, so Jim Smith was a little short of options at right-back. Lee Carsley was also sidelined with a knee injury

A re-shuffle saw Jacob Laursen move to a midfield position and Spencer Prior come into the middle with Derby playing in a 3–5–2 formation, the middle defensive three being Carbonari, Elliot and Prior.

With both teams on a poor run of form, defences were going to be nervous and liable to concede goals. Dean Sturridge, who missed the Liverpool victory through injury,

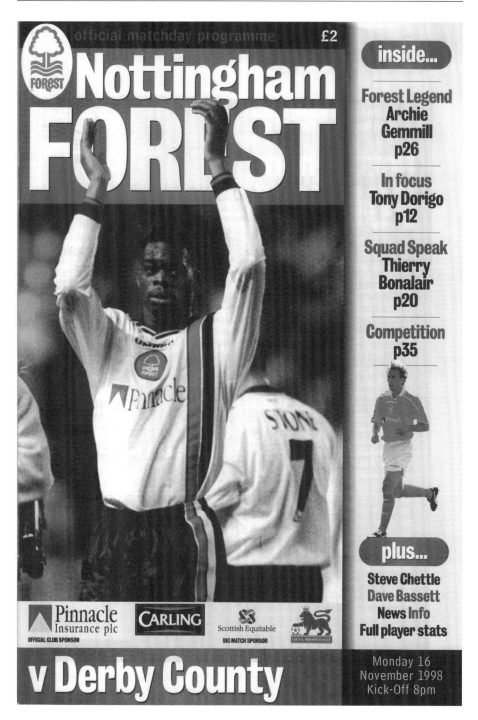

returned to the substitutes' bench giving Kevin Harper another opportunity to build on his Liverpool display.

Russell Hoult was the busier goalkeeper in the first-half, racing out of his goal to block Steve Stone's shot as early as the fifth minute and then diving as Nigel Quashie sent two shots from outside the Derby area just wide of the left-hand post.

Both teams had penalty appeals turned down. Darryl Powell was sent sprawling as Beasant dived at his feet in the 20th minute, and although there was a suspicion of a dive the referee did not book the Derby player. Forest's appeal was even less likely to be given when Freedman made a theatrical fall when challenged by Carbonari five minutes later

The Derby defence held firm in the first half, with Russel Hoult only making one save of note from a van Hooijdonk free-kick just before the interval. Forest had a free-kick on their left channel, midway inside the Derby half. It was all of 35 yards from goal and would need an exceptional effort to score from this unlikely position. The shot was well struck and on target and heading for the top-right-hand corner of Hoult's goal. The goalkeeper managed to get a hand to it and turn it away for a corner kick. That was Forest's best attempt of the half, while Derby had a looping back post Carbonari header cleared off the line by van Hooijdonk after Dorigo's corner had been flicked on to him. Kevin Harper, who had scored at Liverpool, got a dead leg and had to be replaced by Sturridge before half-time.

The first goal of the game came on 56 minutes and sparked a rush of four goals in a 17-minute spell. A goal-kick from Russel Hoult bounced and bobbled its way out towards Derby's left, and Sturridge nipped in behind Thierry Bonalair and was away. His direct running at pace was always likely to cause problems and, as Chettle came across leaving Wanchope and Burton free in the area, Bonalair made a poor challenge from behind which resulted in Sturridge going down and referee Barber had no hesitation in giving the spot-kick.

Tony Dorigo, the former England international defender who had arrived on loan from Italian side Torino (due to their financial predicament) as their Player of the Year, took the spot-kick in front of the Derby fans. His long run up and calm left-footed kick sent the 'keeper the wrong way, and the ball nestled in the back of the net for his first goal for Derby.

Derby's lead was short-lived as immediately Forest won a corner on Derby's left in front of the Trent End. Steve Stone took the corner and eventually the ball was worked back to Nigel Quashie in a central position and 25 yards from goal. His shot was partially blocked on the edge of the area by Dorigo but he could not take enough pace off the ball to stop it breaking to Dougie Freedman who only had Hoult to beat. His firm shot was within Hoult's range, but he could not hold onto it and Freedman himself followed up to slam it into the net.

Forest were on top now and, following a couple of dangerous corners from Stone that led to more Quashie shots, it was Scott Gemmill's chance to take one from the opposite side. He skimmed a corner into the near-post area where Van Hoodijdonk was the first to react and climbed above his markers Carbonari and Wanchope and squeezed his header into the net off the underside of the bar. That was his first goal since his return and his first Premiership goal for 18 months.

The 62nd-minute goal sparked an unusual celebration as all the Forest players ran to congratulate Gemmill and not the goalscorer, the Forest players getting their own back for the striker's previous actions and comments made against them and the club. A similar fate happened to Stan Collymore in his latter days at Forest.

From being a goal up and looking quite comfortable, Derby were now 2–1 down at their fierce rivals on their home ground. Things got worse for Derby on 72 minutes when a break by the left-back Rogers saw him skip past a Carbonari challenge and fire over a low, dangerous centre into the goal area. Russel Hoult dived in to the boot of Steve Stone to block the ball that was kicked out of play for a throw. Russell Hoult was left unconscious in the penalty area having taken the full force of Stone's shot in the face from close range. He was stretchered off wearing a neck brace, and was detained overnight in the local hospital for observation and a series of X-rays on his neck. He was replaced by the Estonian international 'keeper Mart Poom whose only appearances so far that season were limited to Worthington Cup matches against Manchester City and Arsenal, Hoult being regarded as the number one 'keeper at the club.

The fourth goal in the spell was created by Tony Dorigo. His throw-in deep into the Forest half saw Burton run and play it short back to him. Derby had thrown plenty of players forward, expecting a Dorigo long throw. He crossed the ball early and it was flicked on by Prior. The ball reached Wanchope who mis-kicked when well placed for a spectacular volley, but it helped put the defence off balance and caught Bart-Williams ball watching and not marking Carbonari. The Derby defender came behind Bart-Williams and shot first time and scored with ease for his first goal in Derby colours since his summer transfer from Argentina.

From this point onwards all the chances were to go Derby's way, the best of then falling to Dean Sturridge, and they really should have taken advantage of at least one of them to give them their first win at the City Ground since 1971.

The first attempt was when Forest old boy Lars Bohinen won the ball from van Hooijdonk and broke forwards giving Derby a three on two advantage in players, with

Wanchope to his left and Sturridge to his right. As a covering defender moved towards Bohinen, he played Sturridge in, although from a wide and narrow angle he flashed a shot across the face of the goal. Wanchope arrived at the far post a little late as the ball narrowly missed the post.

The last chance of the game again fell to Sturridge when Daryll Powell did well in the middle of the park to win a couple of hard challenges to prise the ball away from Stone and made a 10-yard pass to Sturridge, who again set off at pace. Faced by two defenders he simply knocked the ball beyond them into the penalty area and used his pace to beat them to it. His first-time shot forced Dave Beasant into a full-length save, and he pushed the ball out for a corner. Wanchope, however, was standing all alone on the penalty spot, and a square ball may have been more productive.

Jacob Laursen much prefers his defensive duties but gave an excellent performance in his midfield role and Carbonari continued his upturn in form following the result at Liverpool and now scoring his first goal. There were other excellent performances from Steve Elliot, Spencer Prior, the midfield pair of Powell and Bohinen and the pace of Sturridge, when he came on, was noticeable.

Dave Bassett, the Forest manager said 'I'm not making excuses, but we lost our momentum after the delay when the 'keeper was hurt.'

Jim Smith expanded on that by saying 'we had Forest on toast in the last 20 minutes, but we just didn't finish them off' and Jacob Laursen agreed, 'the score was 2–2 – we should have won that game'.

Derby won the return match at Pride Park 1–0, thanks, again, to another Carbonari goal. Forest finished bottom of the League at the end of the season and were relegated, and one of their results was the famous 8–1 defeat at home to Manchester United, where substitute Solksjaer scored four goals in the last 10 minutes of the game.

HORACIO CARBONARI

Born: 2 May 1974
Debut v Blackburn Rovers (away), Premier League, 15 August 1998, draw 0–0
Last game v Walsall (home), Division One, 5 October 2002, draw 2–2
First goal v Nottingham Forest (away), Premier League, 16 November 1998, draw 2–2
Bought from: Rosario Central, Argentina
Sold to: Released
Total appearances: 100 + 1 sub, 9 goals
Consecutive games: 19 from 13 March 1999 to 18 September 1999

Carbonari was signed in the summer of 1998 for a fee of £2.7 million with a reputation of a strong centre-half with a bullet like shot. He was not the fastest defender but relied on his reading of the game to be in the right place at the right time. For the first three months he was struggling to settle to life in England and performances on the field showed the strain. His first goal for the club came at Nottingham Forest in a 2–2 draw, and he also scored the winner against them in the return fixture at Pride Park. His fierce shot was rarely seen.

Relegation from the Premier League meant a general tightening of the belts, and Carbonari was one of those players who suffered, being on a high wage playing in a lower League, and he was released in January 2003.

DERBY COUNTY 1
EVERTON 0

Premier League   **Saturday 28 August 1999**

Pride Park Stadium

Derby County: Hoult, Prior, Carbonari, Laursen, Borbokis, Johnson (Eranio 46), Bohinen (Baiano 46), Powell, Schnoor, Delap, Fuertes (Sturridge 71). Subs not used: Poom, Beck.

Everton: Gerrard, Weir, Gough, Dunne, Unsworth, Hutchison, Collins, Barmby (Gemmill 80), Pembridge (Ball 66), Campbell, Jeffers (Cadamarteri 66). Subs Not Used: Ward, Simonsen.

Referee: A. D'urso

Attendance: 26,550

Derby were filled with optimism and confidence following their 5–2 mid-week win against Sheffield Wednesday and it was also the debut of Argentinian striker Esteban Fuertes brought in to help Derby add some fire power up front that they had been lacking since Wanchope had been sold.

Despite that win Derby were still sitting in the relegation places with just that mid-week win the only success in the first five Premier League games of the season. Everton were buoyed by their last two results, a 4–1 win against Southampton and a 4–1 mid-week win against Wimbledon, both at Goodison Park, and were sitting seventh in the table at this early stage of the season.

This weekend fixture was played nearly 30 years to the day since Derby manager Jim Smith first took charge in his managerial career – a massive achievement, not reached by many in the modern game. The referee was Andy D'urso, who was new to the Premier League referees' list and had suffered some criticism from Tottenham Hotspur manager George Graham following his first match the previous week. The inexperience of the referee, combined with his over enthusiasm to follow every letter of the law to impress the Premier League assessors, led to him ruining the game as a spectacle.

Derby started the game in the same manner they had finished at Sheffield on Wednesday night, playing their best football of the season so far. After just two minutes,

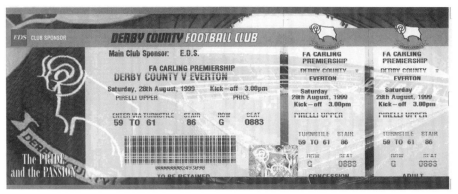

Fuertes, eager to impress on his home debut, charged in from the left hand side and unleashed a shot that the goalkeeper Paul Gerrard could only knock upwards. Rory Delap followed up and his header, despite beating the 'keeper, was headed off the line by Richard Gough.

Richard Dunne, the Republic of Ireland international was booked in the 21st minute for a late challenge on Seth Johnson that sent Johnson spinning into the air. Within five minutes, the same player mistimed a tackle on Derby's left-back Stephan Schnoor that was a little late and high, but it did not really warrant a yellow card. Neither the Derby players or fans were pressurising the referee as a free-kick seemed logical, yet he produced a red card and sent off Dunne. This was Dunne's second red card of his career – not a good record for a 19-year-old defender. It was also Everton's second red card of the season, and their poor disciplinary record in recent seasons saw them fined £50,000 during the summer.

Being reduced to 10 men is not easy at any time, but with 65 minutes to play Everton were up against it and Derby, who traditionally struggle to play against teams in this position, had to find a way round or through the Everton defence, who now would be happy with a 0–0 draw. As Everton re-adjusted their team and formation Derby took control of the game and had several good chances to take the lead. Firstly, Spencer Prior put a Lars Bohinen free-kick over the bar when he really should have done much better.

Fuertes had probably the best of the chances in the first half when he flicked a pass past an Everton defender and ran on powerfully. A shot looked likely to happen, but he passed to Stefan Schnoor who could not keep his shot under control as it flew over the bar. Side-footing the ball instead of trying to break the net would have been the better option as this was the German's best half in English football since his arrival from Germany.

At half-time Jim Smith brought on his two Italians, Stefano Eranio for Seth Johnson and Francesco Baiano for Lars Bohinen who was still recovering from a summer cartilage operation and the large number of games in the opening month. These

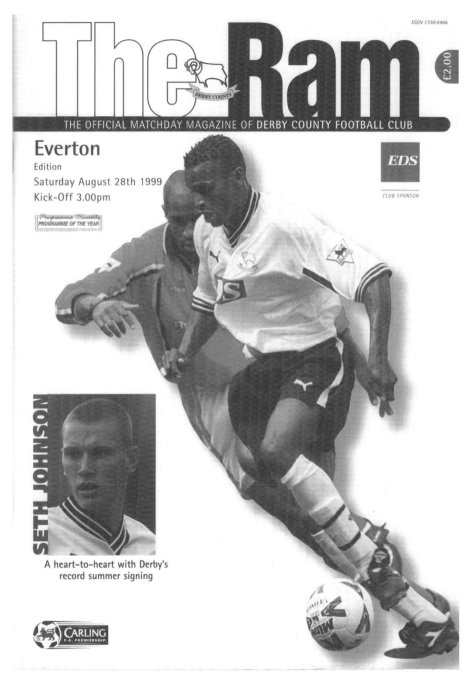

ISSN 1350-8466

The Ram

£2.00

THE OFFICIAL MATCHDAY MAGAZINE OF **DERBY COUNTY FOOTBALL CLUB**

Everton
Edition
Saturday August 28th 1999
Kick-Off 3.00pm

EDS
CLUB SPONSOR

PROGRAMME OF THE YEAR

SETH JOHNSON

A heart-to-heart with Derby's
record summer signing

CARLING
F.A. PREMIERSHIP

changes were to bring a bit more skill into midfield and an extra forward to play up alongside or just behind Fuertes. There were several other yellow cards shown in the first half and the substitution of Johnson was probably precautionary as he had been playing well.

Within 90 seconds of the second half starting, Derby had scored. A short corner was crossed back into the penalty area by Baiano, and Fuertes was left unchallenged by the Everton defence and planted his header with some power past Gerrard from six yards.

Once Derby had scored, they could sit back a little as it was now up to Everton to force the game if they wanted to get anything from it. Derby had several more promising positions, but a poor choice of final ball meant that they were unable to add to their solitary goal, but they seemed to run out of ideas. Everton could muster nothing going forward and Russel Hoult was more or less a spectator. Much of the credit must go to the defensive trio – Carbonari, Prior and Jacob Laursen, although as Everton were playing with 10 men they should have been able to cope.

Everton made a double substitution on 66 minutes with the ineffective Jeffers being replaced by Cadamateri and Ball replacing Pembridge, who received his usual round of boos from the Derby crowd. Fuertes was substituted after 71 minutes, still well short of match fitness, leaving Dean Sturridge slightly startled to be kissed by the Argentinian as they crossed on the touch line.

Everton's only real chance of the game came late in the game as Scottish international John Collins ran at the Derby defence and for once managed to cross the ball. Schnoor could only clear out as far as Don Hutchinson, whose dipping volley from 25 yards skimmed the top of the bar.

The referee would get most of the headlines from this game, effectively spoiling it by the early sending off. In addition to the sending off, he also booked seven other players: Johnson, Fuertes, Carbonari, and Eranio for Derby and Barmby, Gerrard, and Hutchison for Everton. The game itself was not, as that statistic implies, a dirty game, it was physical at times but did not warrant this reaction by the official.

This first home win of the season meant that Derby had won two games in a week, scoring six goals and they had got their new striker involved and scoring early in his Derby career. The complex transfer for Fuertes and his parent club Colon De Santa Fe was into its fifth week, and although the fee of £2.3 million had been agreed various agents still had to be satisfied.

ESTEBAN FUERTES

Born: 26 December 1972
Debut v Sheffield Wednesday (away), Premier League, 25 August 1999, won 2–0
Last game v Liverpool (away), premier League, 6 November 1999, lost 0–2
First goal v Everton (home), Premier League, 28 August 1999, won 1–0

Bought from: Colon de Santa Fe, Argentina

Sold to: Racing Club Lens, France

Total appearances: 10, 2 goals

Consecutive games: 8 from 25 August 1999 to 4 October 1999

Derby were on a pre-season tour of the US in July 1999, and throughout the whole tour the club were in negotiations to bring Fuertes to England as the replacement for Paulo Wanchope. The transfer was very complicated as the player was effectively owned by three groups of people, each with their own agents and representatives. Derby should have pulled out of the transfer and moved to buy a different player.

Eventually clearance was obtained on a £2.3 million deal. Following a training break in Portugal, he was refused entry back into the UK because of a forged Italian passport. This finished his Derby career immediately, but Derby were able to recover their transfer money by selling him to French side Lens, which left Derby a striker short.

DERBY COUNTY 2
WATFORD 0

Premier League   **Monday 3 January 2000**

Pride Park Stadium

Derby County: Poom, Carbonari, Powell, Dorigo (Schnoor), Sturridge (Robinson), Delap, Nimni (Prior), Laursen, Elliott, Burley, Strupar. Subs: Hoult, Schnoor, Prior, Beck, Robinson (M).
Watford: Chamberlain, Page, Palmer, Robinson (P), Ngonge, Hyde, Johnson, Gibbs, Gravelaine, Perpetuini, Miller. Subs: Little, Day, Smith, Bakalli, Foley.
Referee: B. Knight (Orpington)
Attendance: 28,072

With the 21st century into its third day, and no sign of the 'millennium bug' affecting day to day life, the first set of football fixtures in the new millennium was to be played, with Derby at home to Watford in the Premier League.

Derby and Watford were both in the bottom three places in the League table, Watford on 14 points and Derby on 16. Sheffield Wednesday propped up the table on just nine points. Jim Smith was, however, upbeat before the game, his optimism based on recent performances that had brought a win, a draw and a defeat. This was a real 'six-pointer', a game that Derby simply had to win to put some confidence back into the team, to climb out of that bottom three, and put some distance between themselves and Watford.

ISSN 1350-8466

£2.00

The Ram

THE OFFICIAL MATCHDAY MAGAZINE OF DERBY COUNTY FOOTBALL CLUB

Watford
Edition
Monday January 3rd 2000
Kick-Off 3.00pm

CARLING F.A. PREMIERSHIP

PROGRAMME OF THE YEAR

EDS

KINKLADZE

EDS
CLUB SPONSOR

PUMA

Just let those feet do the talkin'
– Giorgi on the high hopes he
has for his Kinky boots

The home form needed urgent attention, with only seven goals scored from the 10 games played and the longer that situation continued, the more pressure would be put on the players not only by themselves, but the management, media and fans, while Watford's last game saw them record a rare victory over Southampton.

Derby's last game of the old millennium was away at West Ham United and the Derby squad was decimated by a flu virus that had ruled out 10 players. This was Watford's first visit to Pride Park Stadium, their last visit being a 1–1 draw in March 1996 in front of just under 16,000 fans at the Baseball Ground. The managers of the two struggling teams needed no introduction to each other as Jim Smith and Graham Taylor played with each other at Lincoln City in the 1960s.

Derby's squad was constantly changing and evolving, with Smith not able to name an unchanged team for some time.

In the latest squad changes:

* Derby had just released Vass Borbokis, for a small fee, back to his native Greece to sign for PAOK Salonika, having been signed in March 1999. He had made just 15 appearances and was not part of the long-term plan.
* Bohinen had been out for three months following a knee operation in September and had managed to play for an hour of the Boxing Day match at West Ham, but was missing from this game due to a family bereavement.
* Seth Johnson was suspended after picking up his 10th yellow card in the win at Leicester two weeks previously, this being the second game of his suspension.
* Stefano Eranio was out with a fractured leg sustained in the defeat at Liverpool, and he would be out for several months to come.
* Lee Morris was due to have a bone graft operation and would be out for the rest of the season.
* Giorgi Kinkladze was not regarded as fully fit.

Rory Delap and Tony Dorigo were back after their bout of flu that had kept them out of the last game and although Strupar had been doubtful with a groin strain sustained against Aston Villa, he was able to play. Avi Nimni was playing his third game and Craig Burley his sixth so there was a good proportion of the team that had not been together long.

Branko Strupar was making only his third appearance for Derby since signing from Belgian club Racing Genk. In the first minute, the game's first opportunity fell to Avi Nimni when he was put in by Rory Delap and Dean Sturridge, but he left it too late to get in a shot and the chance was gone; however, within a minute, Derby were ahead. Tony Dorigo put over a deep cross that Delap managed to get back into the middle where the Watford defence could not get in a clearance and Strupar scored his first goal for Derby, hitting his shot into the top corner. This was Derby's first home goal since 20 November (when Rory Delap scored in the 2–1 defeat to Manchester United), the first goal in the Premier League of the new century, and also the first in British football in the new millennium.

Watford's midfield then took control and gradually created themselves some opportunities, but they really did not trouble Mart Poom. In the main, they would be disappointed that they did not make more of all their possession. Michael Ngonge had a chance to equalise when he went clear from a pass from Charlie Miller. The attempted chip over Mart Poom was an excellent attempt, but the Estonian was able to parry it, and Xavier Gravelaine was unable to make anything of the rebound.

Derby, when they got the ball, looked as if they would score every time they mounted a serious attack. Delap put one shot wide and also fired over a cross through the penalty area without anyone finishing it off. Dean Sturridge headed Strupar's cross against the inside of a post before he picked up a hamstring strain and had to be substituted by Marvin Robinson after 26 minutes, the young striker making his seventh appearance for the club.

Tony Dorigo also had to go off when he injured a calf muscle and was replaced by Stefan Schnoor. Watford were still having trouble stopping Derby creating clear chances – Darryl Powell volleyed wide when a free-kick was not properly cleared; Burley burst through from Strupar's clever knock down to shoot wide of the post; Nimni showing a good piece of skill, forcing Chamberlain to parry a shot.

At half-time, Derby would be pleased to be in front (a rare occurrence) but unhappy with the amount of possession Watford had been given and needed to get tighter on their midfield players. Avi Nimni, only playing due to the list of injuries, seemed to be the biggest culprit as he struggled in this relegation dog-fight. In his first couple of games, he had shown some good touches and running, but now he wanted too much time on the ball and was being caught.

In the second half, both teams huffed and puffed and generally cancelled each other out, and it was not until the latter stages that the result became safe. Local boy, Marvin

Robinson was crudely fouled by Robert Page on 72 minutes, who was rightly booked for the challenge, and although the free-kick was in the range of Horacio Carbonari, Strupar took over. Carbonari's reputation for a lethal and powerful deadball kick was rarely seen and was probably a known threat from Watford's point of view. Strupar curled his shot into the net and showed why Jim Smith took a chance on the Belgian international player.

With less than 20 minutes to go, the second goal was important, and the crowd could relax a little as it was unlikely Watford could stage a recovery and score the two goals required to get a point from the game.

The win took Derby out of the bottom three for the first time since they won against Chelsea in October and gave them just their third home victory of the season. It was the springboard for a good little run of form that saw just one defeat from the next seven games and four defeats from 12 games, those being the away games at Everton, Manchester United, Liverpool and Aston Villa.

Strupar, was now off the mark and showing some good, skilful touches, but he was now unavailable for the next three matches as a suspension from the Belgian FA was carried forward and would take effect before the next game. Avi Nimni was on loan from Israeli club Maccabi Tel Aviv and this was to be his last full game and his last appearance at Pride Park. He had some good touches but sometimes wanted too much time on the ball, which was probably not suited to the pace of the Premier League.

Watford were to finish bottom of the table at the end of the season, some 12 points away from safety.

BRANKO STRUPAR

Born: 9 February 1970
Debut v Leicester City (away), Premier League, 18 December 1999, won 1–0
Last game v Mansfield Town, League Cup, 10 September 2002, won 3–1
First goal v Watford (home), Premier League, 3 January 2000, won 2–0
Bought from: Racing Genk, Belgium
Sold to: Released
Total appearances: 34 + 9 subs, 16 goals
Consecutive games: 12 from 23 February 2002 to 11 May 2002

Although born in Croatia, Branko was able to play international football for Belgium through marriage and was capped 17 times. He won a number of domestic honours in

Belgium – League's top scorer, Player of the Year and had helped his club side to the League title in 1998–99 before his £3 million transfer to Derby in December 1999. During his time with The Rams, there was often a group of Genk supporters to cheer him on at Derby home games.

His goalscoring ratio was excellent (at Genk he had scored 61 goals in 110 appearances), but he was plagued by a series of injuries which limited his availability to just 34 starts in under two years and was costly on a per-game basis. An agreement was made with him and his contract was cancelled.

BRADFORD CITY 4
DERBY COUNTY 4

Premier League   **Good Friday 21 April 2000**

Valley Parade

Bradford City: Clarke, McCall, Weatherall, Westwood, Blake, Beagrie, O'Brien, Windass, Halle, Dreyer, Jacobs. Subs: Todd, Sharpe, Rankin, Saunders, Davison.
Derby County: Poom, Carbonari, Powell, Dorigo, Johnson, Delap, Christie, Laursen, Elliott, Burley, Strupar (Kinkladze). Subs: Oakes, Schnoor, Jackson, Kinkladze, Riggot.
Referee: A.B Wilkie (Chester-le-Street)
Attendance: 18,276

Unusually for an Easter holiday fixture, this one was arranged for Good Friday with a beamback to Pride Park for those not wanting to make the trip to West Yorkshire, or unable to get a ticket. It was a game that neither club could afford to lose, Bradford (managed by Paul Jewell) because they were in the bottom three and facing relegation with five games to go and Derby to stop themselves from being dragged into the relegation dog-fight.

The importance of the game for both teams meant that it was likely to be a tense match with the possibility of lots of mistakes. As the game unfolded it became clear that it was going to be one of those games where defenders seemed to forget how to do the basic things and every attack had the possibility of creating a goal-scoring opportunity.

The tone of the game was set straight from the kick-off when Derby's first attack ended up in the net while the fans were still filing in and getting to their seats. It was timed at 21 seconds when Daryll Powell ran down the left on a pass from Strupar, and his shot was not held by the goalkeeper, Clarke, who could only push it out as far as Malcolm Christie. Christie was in no position to shoot himself but was able to fire

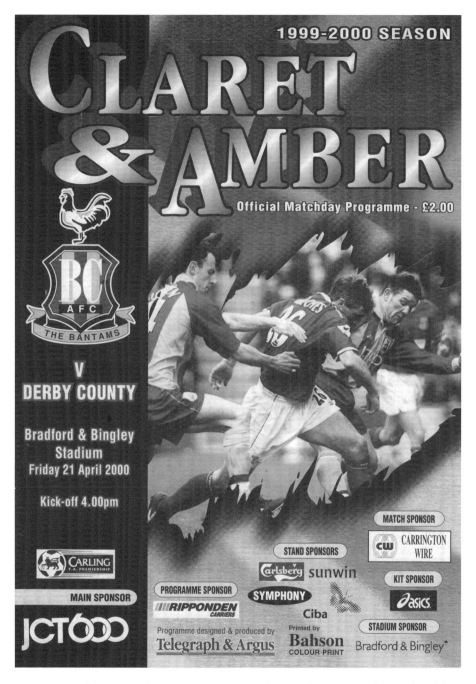

over a centre for Rory Delap to tap in to give Derby a perfect start on the one hand, but still with over 89 minutes to play.

On seven minutes, the situation for Derby got even better with Branko Strupar scoring his fifth goal of the season direct from a free-kick on the edge of the area following a foul on Christie, bending the ball into the bottom corner of the net. At 2–0, it was important that Derby kept their own goal intact for at least the next 20 minutes of the game, to slow the pace of the match down and quieten the home crowd and effectively kill the game. That plan lasted for less than five minutes before Bradford's leading scorer Dean Windass shot from an angle such that the ball squeezed between Poom and the post.

On 18 minutes Windass dragged Bradford level. He picked up a wayward header from Steve Elliott and fired a stunning shot from 35 yards that skidded along the wet turf into the net. Just as Derby had run into a 2–0 lead in seven minutes, Bradford themselves had now scored two in seven minutes to pull themselves level and in the ascendancy.

On 27 minutes, a controversial decision threatened to turn the game in Bradford's favour, and the referee upset all the players and both sets of fans at the same time. A Stuart McCall free-kick was worked through to Robbie Blake, who scored as Valley Parade erupted. Their joy was short lived as the referee had already blown for a shirt pull on the forward by Delap. After consultation with the assistant referee it was decided he had stopped a goalscoring opportunity (strange decision as Blake actually scored) and sent Delap from the field and awarded the penalty. Peter Beagrie scored the resulting penalty and Bradford were ahead for the first time.

Derby continued to press forward, and Christie should have had a penalty when he was tripped in the area, but he did not have long to wait for a positive decision. Ten minutes later Derby also won a penalty, as Christie closed in on Strupar's knock down and was hacked down by Ashley Westwood who was making his first Premiership appearance. Westwood was booked, although it is difficult to understand why he was not also sent off. Craig Burley was the Derby penalty taker and made no mistake with a confident strike.

Malcolm Christie tried again for a penalty and this time the referee had had enough and considered this and the previous incident were dives and booked him before Dean Windass scored again to complete his hat-trick and give Bradford the lead again. Unfortunately for the Derby fans, all the Bradford goals were scored at their end.

A breath-taking first 45 minutes had seen seven goals, two penalties, a hat-trick and a sending-off. The interval was probably not long enough for the managers to go through all of the incidents, changes, and plans for the second half. It was never likely to be a repeat of the first half, with the interval giving everyone chance to calm down and re-organise. Derby had to continue going forward, even with 10 men, as defeat would have left them in serious relegation trouble.

Referee Wilkie was again the centre of attention as on 52 minutes he gave a second penalty to Derby following a clear hand ball from John Dreyer. Burley again took the kick and blasted it past Clarke, and it was all square again at 4–4 with still nearly 40 minutes left to play.

Bradford, still with the man advantage, and Derby tiring, threw on Dean Saunders, a well-known figure to Derby fans from nearly a decade previously. Meanwhile, Derby brought on Kinkladze in place of Strupar, hoping the extra pace and skill could find an opening.

As Bradford tried to battle back, throwing on forwards like confetti, Horacio Carbonari grew in stature. He was terrific, and Derby worked so hard that Bradford failed to make the extra man count. It was Derby, though, who created chances again – firstly, Christie ran through the middle and rounded the 'keeper but O'Brien got back to clear off the line. Then Johnson was put clear by Kinkladze but dragged his shot wide with just the 'keeper to beat.

Derby's chance to win the game came when they were awarded the fourth penalty of the game when Chris Powell appeared to be fouled by Gunnar Halle. This gave Burley the chance to claim his own hat-trick, and a rare one at that, all being penalties. There may have been some indecision in his mind as he stepped up to take it in front of the Derby fans – does he place it left, right, down the middle, or hit and hope? Combine that with where he put the first two, and it may have been better to let someone else take the responsibility. Clarke tipped the ball over the bar. And in the last minute of injury-time, Mart Poom made a marvellous point-blank save from Dean Saunders. To lose the game at that point would have been unfortunate and hard to take.

The result left Bradford down in 19th place in the division some five points from safety with just four games to go, while Derby remained in 16th place some seven points behind Southampton in 15th. Bradford City were banking on their last three home League games against Southampton, Derby and Wimbledon to avoid relegation. They had taken only one point from the first two and were worried

Conceding four goals in a game is never good at any time, but to let in four in the first half alone would have given cause for concern to the management, despite the contribution of Carbonari, who got better as the game went on, and Chris Powell on the left. Despite throwing away the two-goal lead, they still should have won the game in the second half, with the clear chances created for Johnson and Christie and the two penalties. The good thing was that they kept going and searching for a winner despite having only 10 players on the field.

Bradford went on to win three out of those four games, including a final day 1–0 win over Liverpool to scramble out of the bottom three, sending Watford, Sheffield

Wednesday and Wimbledon to Division One. The determination they showed against Derby when coming from 2–0 down, together with a tightening up in defence pulled them through, for another season at least.

CRAIG BURLEY

Born: 24 September 1971

Debut v Leeds United (home), Premier League, 5 December 1999, lost 0–1

Last game v Ipswich Town (Division One), 4 May 2003, lost 1–4

First goal v Middlesborough (away), Premier League, 15 January 2000, won 4–1

Bought from: Celtic, Scotland

Sold to: Released

Total appearances: 80, 13 goals

Consecutive games: 11 from 5 December 1999 to 26 February 2000

Burley, a nephew of former Derby manager George Burley, signed for Derby County on 1 December 1999 for £3 million from Celtic, at a time when Branko Strupar and Kinkladze also joined for similar fees to try and pull away from relegation trouble.

A current Scottish international, he was bought to add some experience, gained at Chelsea and more successfully at Celtic, and ability, to the midfield area. He suffered a serious injury in a match against Newcastle United in November 2001 that kept him out of action for a year.

By the time he returned to action Derby had been relegated and John Gregory had been appointed as manager. He was another player on an expensive contract and negotiated a settlement package to release him from his contract in September 2003 and later played for Dundee, Preston and Walsall in the 2003–04 season.

TEAM OF THE DECADE

Choosing the 'Team of the 1990s' causes the same issues that we had to face during the 2009 fans poll during the 125-year anniversary to choose the All-Time Team.

It will be easy to put names in certain positions that everyone will agree on, but others are open to debate and people's recollections of particular players. There were three distinct phases during the 1990s, starting with the Arthur Cox team containing names like Peter Shilton, Mark Wright and Dean Saunders. By the mid-1990s, those players had moved on and been replaced by the likes of Marco Gabbiadini, Russell Hoult and Paul Simpson.

The Premier League then brought a new, probably technically superior, exciting, fitter generation of foreign players – Mart Poom, Stefano Eranio, Francesco Baiano and Paulo Wanchope.

So, how do we come up with a 'Team of the Decade' when you have to look at the decade in isolation and not what happened in those seasons either side of it? Players like Mark Wright and Dean Saunders only played one season in the decade, while Peter Shilton was past his best and these players would probably take their place in the Team of the Decade for the 1980s.

Some of the options the reader will have to deal with while deciding his or her own team are do you choose Peter Shilton, Mart Poom or Russell Hoult? Igor Stimac or Mark Wright? Paul Simpson or Ted McMinn? Chris Powell or Michael Forsyth? Marco Gabbiadini or Paulo Wanchope? These are just a small sample of the decisions the reader must make.

We will go through each playing position, giving the possible choices for that position and then provide some evidence for my final choice. We will choose to play a traditional 4–4–2 formation for our team and also name some substitutes.

Goalkeeper

The decade started with Derby in the top division, and the goalkeeper throughout their last season before relegation was Peter Shilton, with the odd appearance by his long-term understudy Martin Taylor. Shilton held his position until March 1992 until Taylor briefly took over and then Steve Sutton was brought in to provide competition for the number-one position. These two kept the position between them until Taylor's leg break in October 1994, and then Russell Hoult arrived and eventually became first choice. Mart Poom's signing in 1997 kept Hoult on his toes and exchanging the gloves based on form until Poom became the dominant player. Of those five, we can consider Mart Poom, Russell Hoult and Martin Taylor.

Poom and Taylor both won the supporters' Player of the Year trophy during the decade. Poom lies in fourth place in the number of Premier League appearances (83 + 2 subs with Hoult (66 + 1 sub) in eighth place, Martin Taylor lies ninth in the Division One appearance list (86). Overall Russell Hoult (136 + 2 subs) made more appearances than the other two – Taylor on 115 and Poom on 94 + 2 subs.

In terms of clean sheets as a percentage of games played, Poom is out in front on 35 per cent, Martin Taylor in second (27 per cent) and Russell Hoult on 25 per cent. What has to be remembered is that all of Poom's appearances were in the Premier League whereas Taylor and Hoult were a mixture of Leagues.

Taking the latter into account, Mart Poom gets the goalkeeper's jersey.

Defenders

Right

There were many players that filled in at right-back throughout the 1990s, ranging from Mel Sage, Gary Charles, Gary Rowett, Jason Kavanagh through to Jacob Laursen. Sage left part way through the 1991–92 season and Kavanagh, although starting 92 games and a further 35 substitute appearances, never really established himself in the position.

Of the others Gary Charles was excellent, but he lasted 16 months before a big money move to Aston Villa. That really leaves the choice between Gary Rowett and Jacob Laursen. Both could play across the back line, and both often featured in the same team. Laursen was a regular Danish international and was signed before the Euro '96 tournament started and was a model professional and very consistent, and the supporters voted him as the 'Player of the Year' for the 1998–99 season. Both could easily fill the right-back or centre-back position, but overall Laursen takes the place.

Left

The left-back position was largely dominated by just two players – Chris Powell and Michael Forsyth. Other players played in that position during the decade were Shane Nicholson, Tony Dorigo, Stefan Schnoor but none of them for long enough to be considered.

Chris Powell was signed by Jim Smith in February 1996 from Southend United and was the Player of the Year for Derby's first season in the Premier League. He missed only a handful of games in two and a half seasons and was sold to Charlton, in most peoples' view at least a season too early, after starting exactly 100 games with two substitute appearances. He lies fifth in the Premier League appearance table. He was an excellent defender who loved to get forward, although he only scored twice, and he made his England debut at Pride Park when Mexico were the opponents.

Michael Forsyth made over 200 appearances in the 1990s, having joined The Rams when Arthur Cox was manager in 1986. He was appointed team captain and led the team out during the two Wembley appearances for the Anglo-Italian Cup and Play-off Final. He could also play effectively in the centre of defence. For his versatility and his additional goal scoring, I choose Michael Forsyth to occupy the number-three shirt.

Centre

With two places up for selection, there are plenty of candidates. The decade began with Mark Wright and Michael Forsyth occupying the positions. Mark Wright probably did not play enough games in the decade to justify a place given the other contenders, and Michael Forsyth has already been included at left-back.

This pair were followed by Simon Coleman and Andy Comyn, and then Craig Short and Darren Wassall. Other players in the centre-half position were Paul Williams, Dean Yates, Igor Stimac, Gary Rowett, Christian Dailly, Jacob Laursen, Spencer Prior, Horacio Carbonari and Steve Elliot.

From those above, the list can be narrowed down to Short, Yates and Stimac, the Croatian defender. He was the only one not to receive the annual supporters' award, but his captaincy, influence and supreme confidence (almost arrogance) were special. It was no coincidence that during the Division One promotion year of 1995–96 the club were struggling, and after his first game (a 5–1 defeat at Tranmere in which he scored) they went on a run of 20 games without defeat. Stimac, therefore, goes into the team.

There is little to choose between Yates and Short, both arriving from Notts County, but Craig Short gets the vote due to his physical presence, and his subsequent playing career at Premier League level at Everton and Blackburn Rovers show his pedigree.

Midfield

Right

Gary Micklewhite was the main right-sided midfielder during the relegation season in 1991, and when he moved on Tommy Johnson filled the role. The latter part of the decade saw the formation change and a number of players filled the right-hand position in midfield. Some of those being Sean Flynn, Robin van der Laan, Stefano Eranio, Rory Delap and Lars Bohinen.

Eranio's background, coming from AC Milan and being an Italian international, is far superior to the other players and his skilful play, constant running and likeable personality puts him in the number-seven shirt, mirroring the thoughts of the supporters in the All-Time team selection.

Left

Out on the left, the choice is really between Ted McMinn and Paul Simpson. McMinn's better days were during the late 1980s and Paul Simpson was one of the players brought in by Arthur Cox during his rebuilding of the team in the early 1990s. Simpson's goalscoring record is exceptional for a wide player, and his eye for goal saw him net 57 times (including hat-tricks against Bristol City, Portsmouth and Tranmere Rovers) during his five years and over 160 starts and over 60 substitute appearances.

A change of formation during the promotion season of 1995–96 meant Simpson played more of a central role, and from then onwards his opportunities became limited and eventually saw him leave for definite first-team football.

Centre

For the two central midfield players my list contains the possible choices: Mark Pembridge, Daryll Powell, Robin van der Laan, Paul Williams, Aljosa Asanovic and Lee Carsley. The Croatian Asanovic is undoubtedly the most accomplished of the set of players, but his defensive duties were often neglected.

Paul Williams started his career as a left-back when he was in the youth team and was converted to a midfield player where he spent a number of seasons before being put at centre-half during the 1993–94 season. He spent the rest of his career at Derby, and then at Southampton and Coventry City at centre-half.

Lee Carsley was another player who came through the youth and reserve teams and was given his opportunity when Roy McFarland was manager. He became a regular Republic of Ireland international, but he really made his name after he moved from Derby to Blackburn Rovers and Everton.

Mark Pembridge was bought from Luton Town and was in the Derby side for three seasons, scoring more than 10 goals in each of those seasons, although he was the penalty taker at the time. He was a small, combative, midfielder who went on to play for the Wales national side while with Derby on the strength of his performances. His tough tackling and hard shot made him one of the first names on the team sheet. His desire to play in the Premier League and the way he went about it upset the Derby fans, and he was subsequently booed every time he made a re-appearance against them afterwards.

Daryll Powell's long stride some times gave the impression he was lazy, but he covered a phenomenal distance during each game covering the space between both boxes. He was Jim Smith's first signing for Derby on his arrival in 1995 and was first choice during his six and a half years at the club. He was also selected for the Jamaican national team and was selected in the France '98 World Cup squad.

Robin van der Laan was another one of Smith's first signings and was appointed captain straight away. His drive and leadership through the promotion season was outstanding and he also scored the promotion-clinching goal. Once in the Premier League, his selection was not automatic, and he left at the end of the 1997–98 season after making just 22 Premier League appearances in two seasons.

My own preference is for a midfield that can get up and down the field throughout a game and have a ball winner in the middle. The ball-winner role comes to a selection between Pembridge and Carsley, of which Pembridge with his superior scoring ability gets selected.

The other player to complete the midfield is Daryll Powell.

Forwards

Some of the forwards available for selection are Paulo Wanchope, Marco Gabbiadini, Dean Sturridge, Paul Kitson, Deon Burton and Tommy Johnson. Others such as Francesco Baiano, Ashley Ward, Malcolm Christie, Esteban Fuertes, Branko Strupar, Bobby Davison and Lee Mills did not really play enough games to justify inclusion, although the goals-per-game ratio of some of those (Davison, Ward, Mills and Strupar) are impressive. There are three main contenders for the two places available – Wanchope, Sturridge and Gabbiadini.

Wanchope, as mentioned elsewhere, was very unpredictable but terrified even the best defences in the Premier League, with an excellent scoring record. His debut goal at Old Trafford was the number-one, all-time Derby goal and showed the pace, control and scoring ability that he could produce.

Macro Gabbiadini was a prolific goalscorer for Derby, scoring more than 10 goals in four successive seasons, and was a major influence in the promotion season with his power and strength. He did not manage to reproduce his scoring feats in the top division, and there were games where he struggled but some where he was outstanding.

Dean Sturridge is an automatic choice for the team – his scoring in both Division One and Premier League shows his capability to perform at the highest level, and at one stage there was talk of a multi-million pound transfer away from Derby. His pace was his greatest asset. He scored many memorable goals – the opening goal in the Crystal Palace game (leaving the defence behind and placing his shot into the corner from the edge of the penalty area), the first goal against Leeds United (a neat turn and volley) in the Premier League and his goal at Highbury against Arsenal (cut in from the touchline before unleashing an unstoppable shot past the England goalkeeper David Seaman) among his best.

Wanchope and Sturridge formed a successful partnership when they played together in the Premier League, scoring 27 goals between them in the 1997–98 season and are selected, with Gabbiadini making the substitutes' bench.

Manager

The decade began with Arthur Cox in charge and, after managing the club to its only relegation, he resigned at the start of October 1993 and was replaced by his assistant, Roy McFarland. McFarland guided his team to the 1994 Play-off Final but was not offered another contract at the end of the 1994–95 season.

After interviewing people like Barry Fry and Brian Horne, Jim Smith was tempted away from his desk job at the League Manager's Association, and he remained manager throughout the rest of the decade. Arthur Cox re-built his team with Lionel Pickering's money and reached the Play-off semi-finals and the Final of the Anglo-Italian Cup. Roy McFarland's team reached the Play-off Final but could not progress any further.

Jim Smith had to assemble a squad on his arrival during the close season, losing Short, Williams and Pembridge on his arrival. He bought new players and guided the team to promotion in his first season, the move to Pride Park Stadium, and also he was responsible for bringing in foreign talent like Eranio, Poom, Laursen, Baiano, Wanchope, Stimac, Carbonari, Asanovic as well as Seth Johnson, Robbie van der Laan, and Chris Powell. He secured the reserve-team coach at Oxford United, giving him a start in coaching at the highest level. The coach in question was Steve McClaren, the future England manager. The partnership worked wonderfully well. Things started to go wrong for Derby in the Premier League when McClaren left to join Manchester United during their treble season of 1998–99. A succession of coaches and assistant managers failed to have the same impact as McClaren, and Derby's results showed as they struggled to maintain the status.

Team of the Decade line-up

1
Mart Poom

2
Jacob Laursen

3
Michael Forsyth

5
Craig Short

6
Igor Stimac

7
Stefano Eranio

11
Paul Simpson

4
Mark Pembridge

8
Daryll Powell

9
Paulo Wanchope

10
Dean Sturridge

Substitutes

Russell Hoult

Gary Rowett

Paul Williams

Lee Carsley

Marco Gabbiadini

Manager

Jim Smith

STATISTICS OF THE DECADE

Official Player of the Year

1990–9	Dean Saunders	1995–96	Dean Yates
1991–92	Ted McMinn	1996–97	Chris Powell
1992–93	Marco Gabbiadini	1997–98	Francesco Baiano
1993–94	Martin Taylor	1998–99	Jacob Laursen
1994–95	Craig Short	1999–2000	Mart Poom

Players of the 1990s (Goals in brackets)

	Anglo-Italian	Division One	Division Two	FA Cup	League Cup	Play-off	Premier League	Zenith Data Cup	Total
Aljosa Asanovic				3	2		37+1 (7)		42+1 (7)
Ian Ashbee		1							1
Francesco Baiano				5 (3)	6		52+12 (16)		63+12 (19)
Mikkel Beck				0+1	2		11+7 (2)		13+8 (2)
Chris Boden		8+2							8+2
Paul Boertien					0+1		0+3		0+4
Lars Bohinen				3	2		46+8 (1)		51+8 (1)
Vasillis Borbokis				1	3 (1)		9+7		13+7 (1)
Marc Bridge-Wilkinson							0+1		0+1
Robert Briscoe		2+1			3				5+1
Craig Burley				1			18 (5)		19 (5)
Deon Burton				7+1 (3)	2+1		41+27 (16)		50+29 (19)
Nigel Callaghan		12 (1)						1 (1)	13 (2)
Matt Carbon		2+4		0+1	1		9+5		12+10
Horacio Carbonari				5	1		57+1 (7)		63+1 (7)
Lee Carsley	3	53+5 (3)		12	10+3		69+11 (2)		147+19 (5)
Martyn Chalk			4+3 (1)	3 (1)				0+1	7+4 (2)
Gary Charles	6	61 (3)		1	5+1	3			76+1 (3)
Malcolm Christie					0+1		10+13 (5)		10+14 (5)
Simon Coleman	9	19+8	43 (2)	5	5+1	2		1	84+9 (2)
Andy Comyn	6 (1)	13+4	46 (1)	3+1 (1)	7	2 (1)		1	78+5 (4)
Kevin Cooper	0+1	0+2			0+2				0+5
Gordon Cowans	2+1	36			3	3 (1)			44+1 (1)
Steve Cross		19+2	0+4	1	1			1	22+6
Christian Dailly				4+1	6		62+5 (4)		72+6 (4)
Jonathon Davidson		2+3	1	0+2				0+1	3+6
Will Davies	0+1	1+1							1+2
Bobby Davison			10 (8)						10 (8)
Rory Delap				1+1	5 (1)		65+5 (8)		71+6 (9)
Tony Dorigo				4 (2)	4		37+4 (1)		45+4 (3)
Steve Elliot				2+2	6+1		28+6		36+9
Stefano Eranio				5 (1)	4		58+9 (5)		67+9 (6)
Sean Flynn		29+13 (2)		3	3		10+7 (1)		45+20 (3)
Michael Forsyth	12 (1)	124+2 (3)	43 (1)	9+1	18 (1)	5		3	214+3 (6)
Kevin Francis		0+2		1					1+2
Esteban Fuertes					2 (1)		8 (1)		10 (2)
Marco Gabbiadini	11+1 (6)	138+16 (44)	20 (6)	8+1 (3)	13 (7)	5 (2)	5+9		200+27 (68)
Phil Gee		1+1	17+2 (1)	2+1 (2)	3+1 (1)			1	24+5 (4)
Richard Goulooze	3 (1)	7+5		1	0+1				11+6 (1)
Mick Harford		36 (8)	6 (3)	1	5 (3)			2	50 (14)
John Harkes	3 (1)	67+7 (2)			5	3			78+7 (3)
Kevin Harper				0+3 (1)	1+5		6+26 (1)		7+34 (2)
Steve Hayward	2+3	11+5 (1)	3+4	1	0+2	0+1		1	18+15 (1)
Trevor Hebberd		12+9 (1)			3			2	17+9 (1)
Steve Hodge	1 (2)	10 (2)							11 (4)
Glynn Hodges		1+8							1+8

	Anglo-Italian	Division One	Division Two	FA Cup	League Cup	Play-off	Premier League	Zenith Data Cup	Total
Russell Hoult		55+1		7	8		66+1		136+2
Jonathan Hunt				0+3	2+2		7+18 (2)		9+23 (2)
Richard Jackson							0+2		0+2
Seth Johnson				0+1	1+1		36 (1)		37+2 (1)
Tommy Johnson	11 (4)	79+7 (28)	12 (2)	5 (1)	9+1 (2)	5 (4)			121+8 (41)
Jason Kavanagh	4+7	52+22 (1)	22+3	7	3+2	2+1		2	92+35 (1)
Giorgi Kinkladze				1			12+5 (1)		13+5 (1)
Paul Kitson	11 (9)	93 (32)	12 (4)	5 (1)	7 (3)	2+1			130+1 (49)
Robert Kozluk				2+1	3		9+7		14+8
Martin Kuhl	4 (1)	68 (1)		6	6				84 (2)
Brian Launders							0+1		0+1
Jacob Laursen				7	9		135+2 (3)		151+2 (3)
Paul McGrath				2			23+1		25+1
Ted McMinn	6	19+13 (2)	35+2 (2)	3+1	4	2 (1)		1	70+16 (5)
Gary Micklewhite	1+2	39+2 (2)	28+4 (2)	0+1	8+1 (1)	0+1		2 (1)	78+11 (6)
Lee Mills		16 (7)							16 (7)
Lee Morris							2+1		2+1
Adam Murray							1+11		1+11
Shane Nicholson	5	73+1 (1)		4 (1)	4				86+1 (2)
Avi Nimni				1			2+2 (1)		3+2 (1)
Ian Ormondroyd			25 (8)	3 (1)	3				31 (9)
Paul Parker					2		4		6
Mark Patterson	3 (2)	23+6 (1)	8+4 (2)	4	3+1			1+1	42+12 (5)
Mark Pembridge	12 (5)	108+2 (28)		6 (3)	9 (1)	3			138+2 (37)
Justin Phillips		3 (1)							3 (1)
Nick Pickering		12+1	0+1	1	4			2	19+2
Mart Poom				5	6		83+2.		94+2
Chris Powell		19		5 (1)	6		70+2 (1)		100+2 (2)
Daryll Powell		37 (5)		7+1	6+1		100+20 (3)		150+22 (8)
David Preece		10+3 (1)			2				12+3 (1)
Spencer Prior				4	5		47+6 (1)		56+6 (1)
Andy Quy					0+1				0+1
Marino Rahmberg							0+1		0+1
Craig Ramage		18+5 (1)	7 (2)	1+1	5 (2)	0+1		0+1	31+8 (5)
Kevin Ratcliffe		6							6
Chris Riggott							0+1		0+1
Marvin Robinson							3+6		3+6
Stephen Round		6	2+1						8+1
Gary Rowett		34+1		5+2	8 (2)		67+3 (3)		114+6 (5)
Melvyn Sage		33+1 (1)	17	1	5+1			2	58+2 (1)
Dean Saunders		38 (17)		1	5 (3)			2 (1)	46 (21)
Stefan Schnoor				3	2+1		43+10 (3)		48+11 (3)
Peter Shilton		31	31	4	8			1	75
Craig Short	4	118 (9)		7 (4)	11	3			143 (13)
Paul Simpson	9+2 (2)	117+33 (39)	16 (7)	4+4 (1)	12+3 (6)	5	1+19 (2)		164+61 (57)
Mauricio Solis					1+2		3+8		4+10
Mark Stallard	2 (1)	17+7 (2)	2+1	2+2	2+1 (2)			1 (1)	26+11 (6)
Igor Stimac		27 (1)		7	2		57 (2)		93 (3)
Branko Strupar							13+2 (5)		13+2 (5)
Dean Sturridge	2+1	48+13 (21)	1	8 (2)	9+2 (4)		90+24 (30)		158+40 (57)
Steve Sutton	9	50+1	10	3	7	2			81+1
Wayne Sutton		4+3		1					5+3
Martin Taylor	6	86	5	5	5	3	3	2	115
Paul Trollope		30+11 (4)		3+1	3+2 (1)		17+7 (1)		53+21 (6)
Robin Van der Laan		39 (6)		3+1 (3)	6+2		22+4 (2)		70+7 (11)
Paulo Wanchope				4	6+1 (5)		65+7 (23)		75+8 (28)
Ashley Ward		5+2 (1)		2 (1)	1+1		27+6 (10)		35+9 (12)
Darren Wassall	11	90+8		4	9				114+8
Alex Watson		5							5
Simon Webster		3							3
Ron Willems		31+2 (11)		4+2 (2)	2 (1)		10+16 (2)		47+20 (16)
Geraint Williams		31	39 (2)	3	6			1	80 (2)
Paul Williams	7+1 (2)	103+6 (12)	41 (13)	8 (3)	10+2 (2)	5		2	176+9 (32)
Ian Wilson		11							11
Darren Wrack		4+22 (1)		0+2	0+3				4+27 (1)
Mark Wright		37		1	5			1	44
Dean Yates		49 (3)		3	3		16+3		71+3 (3)

Player Apperances by Season

	1990–91	1991–92	1992–93	1993–94	1994–95	1995–96	1996–97	1997–98	1998–99	1999–2000	Total
Aljosa Asanovic							38 (6)	4+1 (1)			42+1 (7)
Ian Ashbee					1						1
Francesco Baiano								33+3 (13)	23+5 (6)	7+4	63+12 (19)
Mikkel Beck									6+1	7+7 (1)	13+8 (2)
Chris Boden					4+2	4					8+2
Paul Boertien									0+1	0+3	0+4
Lars Bohinen								9 (1)	32+3	10+5	51+8 (1)
Vasillis Borbokis									3+1	10+6 (1)	13+7 (1)
Marc Bridge-Wilkinson										0+1	0+1
Robert Briscoe	5+1										5+1
Craig Burley										19 (5)	19 (5)
Deon Burton							15+17 (3)	20+6 (12)	15+6 (4)		50+29 (19)
Nigel Callaghan	13 (2)										13 (2)
Matt Carbon						2+4	7+5	3+1			12+10
Horacio Carbonari									32+1 (5)	31 (2)	63+1 (7)
Lee Carsley					29+2 (2)	33+4 (1)	20+10	38 (1)	27+3 (1)		147+19 (5)
Martyn Chalk		7+4 (2)									7+4 (2)
Gary Charles				51+1 (1)	25 (2)						76+1 (3)
Malcolm Christie									0+2	10+12 (5)	10+14 (5)
Simon Coleman		52 (2)	30+9	2							84+9 (2)
Andy Comyn		55 (3)	23+5 (1)								78+5 (4)
Kevin Cooper					0+2	0+1	0+2				0+5
Gordon Cowans				22 (1)	22+1						44+1 (1)
Steve Cross	22+2	0+4									22+6
Christian Dailly							37+5 (3)	34+1 (1)	1		72+6 (4)
Jonathon Davidson	2+4	1+2									3+6
Will Davies					1+2						1+2
Bobby Davison		10 (8)									10 (8)
Rory Delap								10+3	24+3 (1)	37 (8)	71+6 (9)
Tony Dorigo									21+1 (3)	24+3	45+4 (3)
Steve Elliot								5+1	9+6	22+2	36+9
Stefano Eranio								25 (5)	24+7 (1)	18+2	67+9 (6)
Sean Flynn						33+13 (2)	12+7 (1)				45+20 (3)
Michael Forsyth	43	52 (2)	58 (2)	36+1 (2)	25+2						214+3 (6)
Kevin Francis	1+2										1+2
Esteban Fuertes										10 (2)	10 (2)
Marco Gabbiadini		22 (7)	59+3 (19)	40+6 (16)	36+2 (13)	37+6 (13)	6+10				200+27 (68)
Phil Gee	1+3	23+2 (4)									24+5 (4)
Richard Goulooze			11+6 (1)								11+6 (1)
Mick Harford	44 (11)	6 (3)									50 (14)
John Harkes				37+2 (3)	34+4	7+1					78+7 (3)
Kevin Harper									6+27 (2)	1+7	7+34 (2)
Steve Hayward	0+1	4+6	8+4 (1)	2+4	4						18+15 (1)
Trevor Hebberd	17+9 (1)										17+9 (1)
Steve Hodge					11 (4)						11 (4)
Glynn Hodges						1+8					1+8
Russell Hoult					15	43+1	36+1	3	26	13	136+2
Jonathan Hunt								9+14 (1)	0+9 (1)		9+23 (2)
Richard Jackson										0+2	0+2
Seth Johnson										37+2 (1)	37+2 (1)
Tommy Johnson		14 (3)	50+1 (10)	38+7 (19)	19 (9)						121+8 (41)
Jason Kavanagh	8+6	26+3	16+3	10+12	22+10 (1)	10+1					92+35 (1)
Giorgi Kinkladze										13+5 (1)	13+5 (1)
Paul Kitson		14 (4)	61 (24)	46+1 (15)	9 (6)						130+1 (49)
Robert Kozluk								9+3	5+5		14+8
Martin Kuhl			40 (1)	32 (1)	12						84 (2)
Brian Launders									0+1		0+1
Jacob Laursen							39+1 (1)	30+1 (1)	44	38 (1)	151+2 (3)
Paul McGrath							25+1				25+1
Ted McMinn	13	44+2 (3)	13+14 (2)								70+16 (5)
Gary Micklewhite	41 (3)	32+5 (3)	5+6								78+11 (6)
Lee Mills					16 (7)						16 (7)
Lee Morris										2+1	2+1
Adam Murray									0+4	1+7	1+11
Shane Nicholson			20 (1)	22 (1)	21	23+1					86+1 (2)

	1990–91	1991–92	1992–93	1993–94	1994–95	1995–96	1996–97	1997–98	1998–99	1999–2000	Total
Avi Nimni										3+2 (1)	3+2 (1)
Ian Ormondroyd		31 (9)									31 (9)
Paul Parker							6				6
Patterson	8+6 (1)	11+5 (2)	23+1 (2)								42+12 (5)
Mark Pembridge			60 (16)	47+2 (11)	31 (10)						138+2 (37)
Justin Phillips	3 (1)										3 (1)
Nick Pickering	19+1	0+1									19+2
Mart Poom							4	41	20+2	29	94+2
Chris Powell						19	40	41+2 (2)			100+2 (2)
Daryll Powell						38+1 (5)	30+6 (1)	15+11	34+4	33	150+22 (8)
David Preece						12+3 (1)					12+3 (1)
Spencer Prior									39+1 (1)	17+5	56+6 (1)
Andy Quy					0+1						0+1
Marino Rahmberg							0+1				0+1
Craig Ramage	21+3 (3)	7+1 (2)	0+1	3+3							31+8 (5)
Kevin Ratcliffe				6							6
Chris Riggott										0+1	0+1
Marvin Robinson									0+1	3+5	3+6
Stephen Round		2+1	6								8+1
Gary Rowett						37+1	40+1 (2)	37+4 (3)			114+6 (5)
Melvyn Sage	39+2 (1)	19									58+2 (1)
Dean Saunders	46 (21)										46 (21)
Stefan Schnoor									25+3 (3)	23+8	48+11 (3)
Peter Shilton	38	37									75
Craig Short			47 (7)	52 (3)	44 (3)						143 (13)
Paul Simpson		18 (7)	40+6 (15)	36+7 (11)	43+6 (9)	24+18 (12)	2+22 (3)	1+2			164+61 (57)
Mauricio Solis							0+2	4+8			4+10
Mark Stallard		4+2 (1)	1+5		17+4 (4)	4 (1)					26+11 (6)
Igor Stimac						28 (1)	23 (1)	24 (1)	18		93 (3)
Branko Strupar										13+2 (5)	13+2 (5)
Dean Sturridge		1	8+2		9+7 (1)	33+6 (20)	33+1 (14)	28+6 (10)	30+6 (5)	16+12 (7)	158+40 (57)
Steve Sutton		12	38		24+1	7					81+1
Wayne Sutton					4+3	1					5+3
Martin Taylor	8	6	26	55	16		4				115
Paul Trollope					23+1 (4)	8+12	16+1 (1)	6+7 (1)			53+21 (6)
Robin Van der Laan						43 (6)	18+3 (5)	9+4			70+7 (11)
Paulo Wanchope							2+3 (1)	36+2 (17)	37+3 (10)		75+8 (28)
Ashley Ward						5+2 (1)	28+6 (11)	2+1			35+9 (12)
Darren Wassall			35	31	31+7	17+1					114+8
Alex Watson	5										5
Simon Webster						3					3
Ron Willems						34+2 (12)	10+9 (4)	3+9			47+20 (16)
Geraint Williams	35	45 (2)									80 (2)
Paul Williams	19+2 (4)	50 (16)	26+2 (6)	37+5 (1)	44 (5)						176+9 (32)
Ian Wilson	11										11
Darren Wrack					2+15 (1)	2+12					4+27 (1)
Mark Wright	44										44
Dean Yates					11 (1)	42 (2)	8+2	10+1			71+3 (3)

Most Premier League Appearances

Name	Played	Substitute	Goals
Jacob Laursen	135	2	3
Daryll Powell	100	20	3
Dean Sturridge	90	24	30
Mart Poom	83	2	0
Chris Powell	70	2	1
Lee Carsley	69	11	2
Gary Rowett	67	3	3
Russell Hoult	66	1	0
Rory Delap	65	5	8
Paulo Wanchope	65	7	23

Most Division One Appearances

Name	Played	Substitute	Goals
Marco Gabbiadini	138	16	44
Michael Forsyth	124	2	3
Craig Short	118	0	9
Paul Simpson	117	33	39
Mark Pembridge	108	2	28
Paul Williams	103	6	12
Paul Kitson	93	0	32
Darren Wassall	90	8	0
Martin Taylor	86	0	0
Tommy Johnson	79	7	28

Top Goalscorers Premier League

Name	Played	Substitute	Goals
Dean Sturridge	90	24	30
Paulo Wanchope	65	7	23
Deon Burton	41	27	16
Francesco Baiano	52	12	16
Ashley Ward	27	6	10
Rory Delap	65	5	8
Horacio Carbonari	57	1	7
Aljosa Asanovic	37	1	7
Craig Burley	18	0	5
Malcolm Christie	10	13	5

Top Goalscorers Division One

Name	Played	Substitute	Goals
Marco Gabbiadini	138	16	44
Paul Simpson	117	33	39
Paul Kitson	93	0	32
Tommy Johnson	79	7	28
Mark Pembridge	108	2	28
Dean Sturridge	48	13	21
Dean Saunders	38	0	17
Paul Williams	103	6	12
Ron Willems	31	2	11
Craig Short	118	0	9

Most FA Cup Appearances

Name	Played	Substitute	Goals
Lee Carsley	12	0	0
Michael Forsyth	9	1	0
Marco Gabbiadini	8	1	3
Dean Sturridge	8	0	2
Paul Williams	8	0	3
Igor Stimac	7	0	0
Russell Hoult	7	0	0
Jacob Laursen	7	0	0
Deon Burton	7	1	3
Daryll Powell	7	1	0

Most League Cup Appearances

Name	Played	Substitute	Goals
Michael Forsyth	18	0	1
Marco Gabbiadini	13	0	7
Paul Simpson	12	3	6
Craig Short	11	0	0
Paul Williams	10	2	2
Lee Carsley	10	3	0
Tommy Johnson	9	1	2
Mark Pembridge	9	0	1
Darren Wassall	9	0	0
Dean Sturridge	9	2	4

Most Anglo-Italian Cup Appearances

Name	Played	Substitute	Goals
Mark Pembridge	12	0	5
Michael Forsyth	12	0	1
Tommy Johnson	11	0	4
Marco Gabbiadini	11	1	6
Darren Wassall	11	0	0
Paul Kitson	11	0	9
Steve Sutton	9	0	0
Simon Coleman	9	0	0
Paul Simpson	9	2	2
Paul Williams	7	1	2

Top Anglo-Italian Cup Goalscorers

Name	Played	Substitute	Goals
Paul Kitson	11	0	9
Marco Gabbiadini	11	1	6
Mark Pembridge	12	0	5
Tommy Johnson	11	0	4
Steve Hodge	1	0	2
Paul Williams	7	1	2
Paul Simpson	9	2	2
Mark Patterson	3	0	2
Richard Goulooze	3	0	1
Michael Forsyth	12	0	1
Martin Kuhl	4	0	1
Mark Stallard	2	0	1
John Harkes	3	0	1
Andy Comyn	6	0	1

Top FA Cup Scorers

Name	Sum of Played
Craig Short	4
Mark Pembridge	3
Deon Burton	3
Francesco Baiano	3
Marco Gabbiadini	3
Paul Williams	3
Robin Van der Laan	3
Tony Dorigo	2
Ron Willems	2
Phil Gee	2
Dean Sturridge	2

Top League Cup Scorers

Name	Played	Substitute	Goals
Marco Gabbiadini	13	0	7
Paul Simpson	12	3	6
Paulo Wanchope	6	1	5
Dean Sturridge	9	2	4
Paul Kitson	7	0	3
Dean Saunders	5	0	3
Mick Harford	5	0	3
Paul Williams	10	2	2
Craig Ramage	5	0	2
Mark Stallard	2	1	2

Playing Summary

Season	Competition	Played	Home W	Home D	Home L	Home F	Home A	Away W	Away D	Away L	Away F	Away A	Pts	Pos	Biggest Home Att	Smallest Home Att	Average Home Att
1990–91	Division 1	38	3	8	8	25	36	2	1	16	12	39	24	20	21729	11680	16380
1990–91	League Cup	5	2	0	1	8	2	0	2	0	2	2			17050	12253	15241
1990–91	Zenith Data Cup	2	1	0	0	1	0	0	0	1	1	2			7270	7270	7270
1990–91	FA Cup	1	0	0	0	0	0	0	0	1	0	2					
1991–92	Division 2	46	11	4	8	35	24	12	5	6	34	27	78	3	22,608	10,559	14,648
1991–92	League Cup	3	0	1	0	0	0	1	0	1	3	2			10,215	10,215	10,215
1991–92	Zenith Data Cup	1	0	0	0	0	0	0	0	1	2	4					
1991–92	FA Cup	3	1	0	1	5	4	0	1	0	2	2			22452	18364	20408
1991–92	Play Off	2	1	0	0	2	1	0	0	1	2	4			22920	22920	22920
1992–93	Division 1	46	11	2	10	40	33	8	7	8	28	24	66	8	21478	12166	15032
1992–93	Anglo–Italian	9	2	0	2	9	7	4	0	1	13	7			14494	6767	9142
1992–93	League Cup	4	1	1	0	8	1	0	0	2	1	3			22208	13328	17768
1992–93	FA Cup	5	2	1	0	8	5	1	0	1	5	2			22511	17960	20253
1993–94	Division 1	46	15	3	5	44	25	5	8	10	29	43	71	6	19300	13370	15936
1993–94	Anglo–Italian	2	1	0	0	3	2	0	0	1	2	3			6654	6654	6654
1993–94	League Cup	3	1	0	1	2	1	1	0	0	3	1			19858	10569	15213
1993–94	FA Cup	1	0	0	0	0	0	0	0	1	1	2					
1993–94	Play Off	3	1	0	0	2	0	1	0	1	4	3			17401	17401	17401
1994–95	Division 1	46	12	6	5	44	23	6	6	11	22	28	66	9	16839	10585	13588
1994–95	Anglo–Italian	4	2	0	0	9	2	0	1	1	2	3			2010	1562	1786
1994–95	League Cup	4	1	0	0	2	0	1	0	2	3	5			9476	9476	9476
1994–95	FA Cup	1	0	0	0	0	0	0	0	1	0	1					
1995–96	Division 1	46	14	8	1	48	22	7	8	8	23	29	79	2	17460	9242	14327
1995–96	League Cup	3	0	1	1	1	2	1	0	0	3	1			16030	8825	12427
1995–96	FA Cup	1	0	0	1	2	4	0	0	0	0	0			16155	16155	16155
1996–97	Premier League	38	8	6	5	25	22	3	7	9	20	36	46	12	18287	17022	17890
1996–97	League Cup	2	0	1	0	2	2	0	0	1	0	1			13569	13569	13569
1996–97	FA Cup	4	2	0	1	6	5	1	0	0	2	0			18033	17567	17859
1997–98	Premier League	38	12	3	4	33	18	4	4	11	19	31	55	9	30492	25625	29104
1997–98	League Cup	4	1	0	1	5	1	2	0	0	3	1			27364	18490	22927
1997–98	FA Cup	2	1	0	0	2	0	0	0	1	0	2			27992	27992	27992
1998–99	Premier League	38	8	7	4	22	19	5	6	8	18	26	52	8	32913	25710	29192
1998–99	League Cup	3	0	1	1	2	3	1	0	0	1	0			25621	22986	24303
1998–99	FA Cup	5	1	0	0	3	1	2	1	1	6	3			28704	28704	28704
1999–00	Premier League	38	6	3	10	22	25	3	8	8	22	32	38	16	33378	24045	29351
1999–00	League Cup	3	1	0	1	4	3	0	1	0	0	0			20242	19152	19697
1999–00	FA Cup	1	0	0	1	0	1	0	0	0	0	0			23400	23400	23400

League Points per Month

Season	Aug	Sep	Oct	Nov	Dec	Jan	Feb	Mar	Apr	May
1990–91	1	2	6	13	17	18	19	20	21	24
1991–92	4	13	25	34	38	39	51	58	75	78
1992–93	1	6	18	24	33	35	44	51	60	66
1993–94	7	11	23	29	36	42	50	56	71	71
1994–95	1	14	17	26	32	39	42	58	66	66
1995–96	2	9	18	28	43	50	60	68	79	79
1996–97	2	10	11	21	23	25	29	35	43	46
1997–98	3	12	17	23	32	39	45	45	49	55
1998–99	3	12	14	21	28	34	38	44	48	52
1999–2000	7	8	12	12	16	23	25	28	37	38

Top Baseball Ground Attendances

Season	Date	Name	Competition	Att	Result	Score
1991–92	13 May 1992	Blackburn Rovers	Play Off	22,920	W	2–1
1991–92	2 May 1992	Swindon Town	Division 2	22,608	W	2–1
1992–93	8 March 1993	Sheffield Wednesday	FA Cup	22,511	D	3–3r
1991–92	5 February 1992	Aston Villa	FA Cup	22,452	L	3–4
1992–93	28 October 1992	Arsenal	League Cup	22,208	D	1–1
1990–91	24 November 1990	Nottingham Forest	Division 1	21,729	W	2–1
1992–93	28 December 1992	Portsmouth	Division 1	21,478	L	2–4
1991–92	20 April 1992	Newcastle United	Division 2	21,363	W	4–1
1990–91	10 November 1990	Manchester United	Division 1	21,115	D	0–0
1991–92	21 March 1992	Wolverhampton W.	Division 2	21,024	L	1–2

1990–91	23 March 1991	Liverpool	Division 1	20,531	L	1–7
1992–93	13 February 1993	Bolton Wanderers	FA Cup	20,289	W	3–1
1993–94	27 October 1993	Tottenham Hotspur	League Cup	19,858	L	0–1
1991–92	30 November 1991	Leicester City	Division 2	19,306	L	1–2
1993–94	27 April 1994	Nottingham Forest	Division 1	19,300	L	0–2
1990–91	15 September 1990	Aston Villa	Division 1	19,024	L	0–2
1993–94	20 April 1994	Notts County	Division 1	18,602	D	1–1
1990–91	30 March 1991	Arsenal	Division 1	18,397	L	0–2
1991–92	25 January 1992	Burnley	FA Cup	18,364	W	2–0
1996–97	11 May 1997	Arsenal	Premier League	18,287	L	1–3

Top Pride Park Attendances

Season	Date	Name	Competition	Att	Result	Score
1999–2000	18 March 2000	Liverpool	Premier League	33,378	L	0–2
1999–2000	20 November 1999	Manchester United	Premier League	33,370	L	1–2
1999–2000	26 December 1999	Aston Villa	Premier League	33,222	L	0–2
1998–99	13 March 1999	Liverpool	Premier League	32,913	W	3–2
1998–99	28 December 1998	Middlesbrough	Premier League	32,726	W	2–1
1999–2000	6 May 2000	Newcastle United	Premier League	32,724	D	0–0
1998–99	8 May 1999	Coventry City	Premier League	32,450	D	0–0
1998–99	10 April 1999	Nottingham Forest	Premier League	32,217	W	1–0
1998–99	3 April 1999	Newcastle United	Premier League	32,039	L	3–4
1998–99	22 November 1998	West Ham United	Premier League	31,366	L	0–2
1999–2000	15 April 2000	West Ham United	Premier League	31,202	L	1–2
1999–2000	25 September 1999	Bradford City	Premier League	31,035	L	0–1
1998–99	24 October 1998	Manchester United	Premier League	30,867	D	1–1
1997–98	10 May 1998	Liverpool	Premier League	30,492	W	1–0
1997–98	7 February 1998	Aston Villa	Premier League	30,251	L	0–1
1997–98	26 December 1997	Newcastle United	Premier League	30,232	W	1–0
1997–98	15 March 1998	Leeds United	Premier League	30,217	L	0–5
1997–98	28 February 1998	Sheffield Wednesday	Premier League	30,203	W	3–0
1997–98	31 January 1998	Tottenham Hotspur	Premier League	30,187	W	2–1
1999–2000	5 February 2000	Sheffield Wednesday	Premier League	30,100	D	3–3

Score Frequency

Score	1990–91	1991–92	1992–93	1993–94	1994–95	1995–96	1996–97	1997–98	1998–99	1999–2000	Total
0–0	2	4	4	3	6	6	4	4	6	5	44
0–1	4	3	7	3	8	4	5	8	5	4	51
0–2	7	4	1	2		1	4	2	2	6	29
0–3	4		1	2		2					9
0–4				2				3		1	6
0–5								1		1	2
1–0	3	4	1	3	4	4	2	4	7	2	34
1–1	8	4	6	5	5	9	6	1	5	3	52
1–2	6	7	9	5	7		1	1	4	6	46
1–3	2		2	1	3		4	1		2	15
1–4				1	1				1		3
1–5						1			1		2
1–6							1				1
1–7	1										1
2–0		6	7	7	4	2	2	3	1	3	35
2–1	3	8	5	5	3	5	5	4	6		44
2–2		3		2	1	2	3	1	4	1	17
2–3	2		2	2	1	2					9
2–4		2	1			1	1				5
3–0		1	4		2	2		2	1	1	13
3–1		3	5	3	3	3	1	3	1	2	24
3–2		2	1	2	1	2	3		1		12
3–3	1		1	1	1		1	1		2	8
3–4		2	1	1				1	1		6
4–0				1	1			2		1	5
4–1		2				2				1	5
4–2			2	1	1	1	1				6
4–3			2	1	1						4
4–4										1	1
4–6	1										1
5–0				1	1			1			3
5–1			1								1
5–2								1			1
5–3				1							1
6–0	1										1
6–1					1						1
6–2	1					1					2
7–0			1								1

Total Appearances 1990–91 to 2000–01

Name	Played	Substitute	Goals
Michael Forsyth	214	3	6
Marco Gabbiadini	200	27	68
Paul Williams	176	9	32
Paul Simpson	164	61	57
Dean Sturridge	158	40	57
Jacob Laursen	151	2	3
Daryll Powell	150	22	8
Lee Carsley	147	19	5
Craig Short	143	0	13
Mark Pembridge	138	2	37
Russell Hoult	136	2	0
Paul Kitson	130	1	49
Tommy Johnson	121	8	41
Martin Taylor	115	0	0
Darren Wassall	114	8	0
Gary Rowett	114	6	5
Chris Powell	100	2	2
Mart Poom	94	2	0
Igor Stimac	93	0	3
Jason Kavanagh	92	35	1

Top goalscorers 1990-2000

Name	Played	Substitute	Goals
Marco Gabbiadini	200	27	68
Dean Sturridge	158	40	57
Paul Simpson	164	61	57
Paul Kitson	130	1	49
Tommy Johnson	121	8	41
Mark Pembridge	138	2	37
Paul Williams	176	9	32
Paulo Wanchope	75	8	28
Dean Saunders	46	0	21
Deon Burton	50	29	19
Francesco Baiano	63	12	19
Ron Willems	47	20	16
Mick Harford	50	0	14
Craig Short	143	0	13
Ashley Ward	35	9	12
Robin Van der Laan	70	7	11
Ian Ormondroyd	31	0	9
Rory Delap	71	6	9
Bobby Davison	10	0	8
Daryll Powell	150	22	8

Substitution appearances

Name	Played	Substitute	Goals
Paul Simpson	164	61	57
Dean Sturridge	158	40	57
Jason Kavanagh	92	35	1
Kevin Harper	7	34	2
Deon Burton	50	29	19
Darren Wrack	4	27	1
Marco Gabbiadini	200	27	68
Jonathan Hunt	9	23	2
Daryll Powell	150	22	8
Paul Trollope	53	21	6
Sean Flynn	45	20	3
Ron Willems	47	20	16
Lee Carsley	147	19	5
Ted McMinn	70	16	5
Steve Hayward	18	15	1
Malcolm Christie	10	14	5
Francesco Baiano	63	12	19
Mark Patterson	42	12	5
Gary Micklewhite	78	11	6
Stefan Schnoor	48	11	3

Goalkeepers Clean Sheets

Name	Clean Sheets	Played	%
Hoult	34	136	25
Poom	33	94	35
Taylor	31	115	27
Sutton	23	81	28
Shilton	15	75	20